...And they danced on.

Special Thanks to those who have helped

Editors: *Deirdre Towers*
Michael Kronenwetter

Art Consultant: *Bill Miller*

Jacket Concept: *Christopher P. Kasper*

Photographer: *Kirk Fleischauer*

Cover Dancer: *Annaluna Karkar*

Make-up Artist (for cover): *Laurie Maegli*

Publishing Consultant: *John Maegli*

Title: *Joseph Possley*

Printer: *Marathon Press*

Aardvark Enterprises, Ltd., *Joseph J. Estermann*, President

*Pat Brown, Bryan Dornstreich, Beverly Folgert, Barbara Newtow*n,
The Performing Arts Foundation (for the use of the Grand Theatre, Wausau,
Wisconsin to prepare the cover photographs), *Josephine Pierce, Janet Ternent
and Linda Ware*.

*This book is dedicated with love to
all the artists who have contributed
to the beauty, harmony and joy in life.*

INTRODUCTION

For me, it is impossible to love dance without loving dancers. I have treasured my private exchanges with dancers over the years, learning their aspirations, consoling and advising them. Because of the intimacy gained over years of post-concert dinners, I heard both the good and the bad. The decorum generally maintained in the face of a journalist was dropped and the bloopers, the near-disasters, the miraculous cover-ups were revealed.

This delightful coffee table book contains just that -- the silly moments that would ordinarily be kept as quiet secrets. Without shaking the artistry of the dancers portrayed, the shared memories bring us closer to artists as people.

WILLIAM COMO
Former Editor- in-Chief, Dance Magazine

PREFACE

On a sunny, cold, winter afternoon, one of my students brought me a dozen, dusty copies of "The American Dancer." She had found the magazines in the attic of an old house.

What a find! I carefully pulled apart the pages that were stuck together. Except for some water stains and brown edges, time had preserved them well. The magazines, dating back to 1936, contained marvelous stories about pioneer dancers.

With my arms full of the treasures, I looked for a place to hide. There was a perfect spot by the window where the sunshine makes its way into our living room. I paused for a moment to look out the window. Outside it was quiet and peaceful. Silver sparkles reflected off the snow that covered our majestic pine tree. It looked as if Mr. Winter had artfully draped his coat over the branches. I relaxed and settled in a chair to stay for a while.

As I read the stories, my curiosity grew about those pioneer dancers, seemingly unearthly creatures. So much glamour and elegance surrounded them. The stories quickly invaded my cozy corner and soon the magazines covered a large space around me. Too soon, the sun created shadows on the hardwood floor -- a sign it was getting late. It was almost time to come back to earth again.

I stretched my arms across the floor to reach for a particular magazine I had laid aside. I turned once more to the pages in which Ms. Irina Baronova shared anecdotes of many seasons gone by.

"Now and again we get some thrill, some excitement behind the scenes," she told the reporter. "When we were performing at the Bournemouth, a dancer's costume caught on fire from a candle flame. What screaming, what shouting! She ran across the stage, flames shooting. Everybody was poof! Up in the air. But the fires were put out and soon all was well." (1)

In the same article, she was reported to have said, "A sense of humor is an asset, a great one, to life in the ballet. It helps to sustain the equilibrium and the equanimity, yes? You like my English! We laugh all the time. There are lots of little jokes between dancers of the company, you understand." (2)

The echoes of the past fascinated me, not only for the magic of the dance, but also because the stories gave me insights into the dancers as people I would otherwise have not known.

I looked up from the paper and thought about dancers I had known personally. I remembered the summer I studied in Switzerland with Joan Lawson of the Royal Ballet. She was one of the most talented, and incredibly delightful teachers I had ever met.

Years later, we invited Ms. Lawson to teach at our school and stay with us for a week. Not only did she sing to our then five-year old daughter Annaluna, but she also helped her with her bath and taught her how to use a butter knife in the English style. She is the author of many books and a renowned teacher, and yet, she folded laundry and matched socks from a basket I had stashed away behind the door! We never expected this elegant lady to have such a homey side.

As I collected stories, I made new friends, and found out more about life behind the scenes. One afternoon I saw Ivan Nagy, one of my favorite dancers, and Gelsey Kirkland perform the *Don Quixote*, pas de deux in Madison, Wisconsin. The curtain rose and there posed the dancers. The taped music started - just a few notes - the audience breathed in anticipation - then abruptly the music came to a halt and so did the dancers. The tape broke and the curtain dropped. After a few more false starts with the tape breaking, the dancers walking on and off, the program began. But during the performance I had the feeling that all was still not well. We also could not see them after the performance.

Sometime later, I asked Ivan about that performance. After a short pause, he laughed and told me that he and Gelsey had another engagement that evening. After their performance, they were rushed out of the theatre in their costumes to a taxi. In the back seat, they changed into their street clothes while the car sped to the airport. They boarded a private jet just in time to be rushed to their next destination. Imagine changing a tutu in the back seat of a moving car!

Then not too long ago, a friend attended a business meeting in New York and invited her young daughter to come along to see *Swan Lake* at the Opera House. During Act II, one of the swans slipped, fell, and landed in a most unbecoming way on her derrière. Her mother told me that her little girl whispered, all too loud, "Mother, she's alive."

When I heard that story, I decided to collect more stories and to compile this book. We see the artist who defies gravity on stage and takes us away from the drudgery of everyday life - the artist who takes us to the world of enchantment. But the artist, of course, is a person subject to hazards and mishaps. It is my goal to share these stories that depict the hidden side of the artist's world.

On a wall in my small office in our large house I have a beautiful photo of Natasha Makarova in *Romeo and Juliet* which she has personally signed for me. Her autobiography rests on a shelf behind my desk and I retain vivid memories of the first time I ever saw her dance. Never before had I seen anyone dance like her. When I asked her many years later if she had a funny story, she laughed and said, "the whole life is funny". By the way, Natasha is married to my husband's cousin, Edward.

My work began to spread its wings and slowly cover all the flat surfaces in our dining room. For weeks on end, the photos and folders of written material took up what looked like, permanent residence.

At times I felt I would never complete this project because few of the artists ever remained in one place for very long.

I chased them all over the globe, at all times of the day and night. Some told me their stories over the phone. Others wrote and sent their pictures, sometimes to be lost in the mail and I had to call again and again. Because of the sensitivity of the project, the stories were edited and examined to retain the integrity of the stories and the artists. Every story in this book of memories is authentic. Each is a chance to know artists as the vulnerable beings they are.

(1) R. Anderson, "Ballerina - To You", <u>The American Dancer</u>, March 1939, pp. 10 - 11
(2) Op. Cit.

Table of Contents

Photo by: Maurice Seymour

RUTH PAGE founded the Ruth Page Foundation School of Dance in Chicago. She began her long career at the age of 15 as a member of Anna Pavlova's company, and later danced with Diaghilev's Ballet Russe de Monte Carlo and the New York Metropolitan Opera. She made her Chicago debut in 1919 as the star of Adolph Bolm's *The Birthday of Infanta*. She first worked as a choreographer with Bentley Stone, with whom she founded the Page-Stone Ballet, (which later became the Chicago Opera Ballet). Ms. Page and Mr. Bentley together performed *The American Pattern* and *Frankie and Johnny*, music for both by Jerome Moross. Ms. Page danced in 1925 the lead role in *Krazy Kat*, ballet score by John Alden Carpenter, and performed by the Chicago Allied Arts in the first "ballet theater" in the United States. In 1928, she was invited to perform at the Imperial Theatre, Tokyo, at the enthronement ceremonies of the Emperor Hirohito. She was the only Westerner to receive the invitation. Her *Merry Widow* ballet, filmed with Peter Martins and Patricia McBride, broadcast on public television, received the prestigious Peabody Award. Ms. Page wrote "Class", a book about her dance classes around the world.

Ruth Page

A TRAUMATIC EXPERIENCE

"...I got off to the wrong start..."

In 1922, I was dancing in Adolph Bolm's *Ballet Intime* at the Berkeley Greek Theatre, doing a solo called *Flight of the Bumble Bee*. I was to be a peasant girl chased by an imaginary bee. The music was difficult and the choreography complicated. As soon as the music began, I got off to the wrong start, forgot all the steps, and made up the whole thing.

I ran around the stage as if possessed. In reality, I was terrified.

After the performance, I cried for hours.

The next day, the review in the newspaper announced "A great new dramatic dancer has arrived!" Well, I fooled them.

Yet, the experience was so traumatic, that I have never forgotten a dance since.

Photo by: Sheila Malkind

Frederic (Freddy) Franklin

PIONEERING

"Imagine -- Alexandra Danilova and Alicia Markova shooting off pistols!"

Following a successful season at London's Covent Garden in 1938, the Ballet Russe de Monte Carlo sailed to the United States for a tour arranged by the famous impresario, Sol Hurok. Our first performance was at the old Met in New York, but after that, we set out across the country. We were the largest company ever to have toured the United States at that time. Touring in those days took patience, endurance, and a sense of humor. But we were pioneers, building an audience for dance, and we had some wonderful adventures. We made many one night stands in cities that had never been exposed before to classical ballet. One of those cities was Phoenix, Arizona. The population was only about 60,000 people then, yet it was growing fast, thanks, we were told, to the rail link completed by the Southern Pacific Railroad in 1926. Still, Phoenix was not far removed from its frontier days, and a strong romance still held its people to the Old West.

The morning after our arrival, the sun was shining and the streets were alive with people. When Alexandra Danilova, Alicia Markova, Igor Youskevitch and I stepped out of our hotel, we were surprised to find a cart and horse at the door with a banner reading "Ballet Russe De Monte Carlo" across its side. "You have to sit in the cart," we were told. It seemed an unlikely means of transportation for a company that had danced for heads of state, much less for such elegant ladies as Alexandra and Alicia. Nonetheless, we climbed aboard.

Then, even more astonishingly, we were handed loaded revolvers. The ladies were terrified at the sight of them. "What are we to do with these?" we asked. Shoot them, of course. Hurok was a great believer in publicity. We had to ride through the streets of Phoenix, firing the guns, to draw people into the theatre for that night's performance. Imagine -- Alexandra Danilova and Alicia Markova shooting off pistols! But they did!

STAGES

"'But we can't dance on it,' I told her. 'We'll break our necks.'"

Most companies carry their own floor. However, in the early days the condition of some of the stages we performed on was horrendous. I remember arriving at one theatre, to find to our horror, that the floor was polished! The lady in charge of the theatre, naively, proudly, said, "Look!", happily pointing to the glistening, treacherous surface. "Isn't it a beautiful stage?"

"But we can't dance on it," I told her. "We'll break our necks. It's too slippery." She was distressed, but I insisted. "The company cannot perform."

Well, we sanded the floor and used all kinds of detergents so that we could, in fact, perform. At least we were grateful that it didn't have a trap door like the one in the stage of the old Met. If you got on one of those things, well, that was it. A pirouette of any kind guaranteed disaster.

THE CURTAIN FALLS

"I was astonished to see the backdrop drifting down..."

On one of our tours through the Midwest, we performed a surprise ending to *Carnival*. The whole company was on stage for the finale when I looked up and was astonished to see the backdrop drifting, slowly and gracefully down to the stage. Within a few seconds, the enormous canvas descended remorselessly upon us. There was nothing anyone could do. We continued dancing until we were entirely covered by the monstrous cloth. What the audience thought, I don't know -- but we thought it was marvelous!

MARIA TALLCHIEF is recognized as America's first great prima ballerina. The daughter of a chief of the Osage tribe, she was born in Fairfax, Oklahoma in 1925. She chose a ballet career at the age of fifteen. After finishing high school, Ms. Tallchief joined the Ballet Russe de Monte Carlo and quickly rose to soloist status. She married George Balanchine in 1946, and when he formed the New York City Ballet in 1949, she became that company's prima ballerina. In 1953, she received "The Woman of the Year Award" from President Eisenhower. Set to the Stravinsky score, *Firebird* was created for her unique artistry and technical talents and it became her most exciting role. In 1974, Ms. Tallchief established a ballet school for the Lyric Opera of Chicago. From that school, she developed the Chicago City Ballet. She is an avid football fan and roots for the Chicago Bears.

Maria Tallchief

A NEW PARTNER

"I could tell by the expression on his face that he was frightened to death."

George Balanchine choreographed *Scotch Symphony* for me in 1952. It premiered in New York City that same year, with André Eglevsky as my partner.

André was unable to dance one night, and a young dancer was picked to take his place. The young man was relatively inexperienced and extremely nervous.

In the beautiful adagio of the second movement, dressed in a long, romantic tutu, I was thrown through the air by two strong men. Like a bird, I sailed over the stage to be caught by André. Only on this night, it was not André who waited, but my new partner.

My poor new partner.

As I soared towards him, I could tell by the expression on his face that he was frightened to death. And with good reason.

He caught me, but the force of my flying body knocked him off balance. He stumbled backwards toward the edge of the stage. We found ourselves in a heap down by the footlights, all tangled up in the fabric of my beautiful tutu.

I felt sorry for him as we pulled ourselves from my costume. Of course, we finished the ballet as though nothing had happened.

IVAN NAGY, born in Debrecen, Hungary, received his early ballet training from his mother. After winning a silver medal at the Varna International Ballet Competition, he joined the Budapest State Opera Ballet in 1960. He was discovered by Frederic Franklin in 1965, and came to the United States, where he performed with Mr. Franklin's National Ballet, in Washington, D.C., New York City Ballet, and American Ballet Theatre. After retiring as a performer, Mr. Nagy guest-directed and staged works for American Ballet Theatre, as well as for the Australian Ballet, the Hong Kong Ballet, the Puerto Rico Ballet de San Juan, and the Darvash Ballet School in New York. He also served as artistic director of the Ballet del Teatro Municipal in Santiago, Chile, for five years before assuming his current position as artistic director of the Cincinnati Ballet.

Ivan Nagy

CUSTOMS AND MORES

"Even though I was nauseous , throwing up between performances, I still managed to dance ...."

After my first season with the American Ballet Theatre at the Metropolitan Opera in New York, I joined the company, in September 1968, for a three week tour through Japan.

There was much to adjust to, especially the food. Being brought up in Hungary, I had not been exposed to seafood and was reluctant to be now. I tried to survive on rice alone. My strength left quickly, and I felt ghastly, to say the least. In desperation, I began to eat all kinds of raw fish, but my experiments were most discouraging.

Being new with the company, I was nervous and did my very best to please Lucia Chase, our director. Even though I was nauseous, throwing up between performances, I still managed to dance every day.

One of the ballets I performed was *Etude*. The first boy in line, I was always worried about my *tour en l'air*, and I developed a terrible complex about that section of the music. Then one day I jumped in the air, fell off balance, struggled to land on two feet, but nearly ended up in the orchestra pit. After this terrifying performance, Lucia Chase stormed into my dressing room. "I must talk to you, young man," she said. Before she said anything more, I quickly apologized. "I am terribly sorry, Madame Chase," I began. [My European background would not allow me to call her anything less formal than "Madame Chase".] "I have to admit," I continued, speaking all in one breath. "I almost fell into the orchestra pit. I am ill. I can't eat. I have no energy, and I am dancing everyday."

She stood quietly for a moment. "Ivan," she said, ignoring my protests "your hair is much too long. You've got to get a shag."

I sighed with relief. She was only concerned about my sixties haircut.

By the time we left Japan, I could not decide what was my greatest accomplishment -- eating raw fish, living with my new hairstyle, or calling Madame Chase simply "Lucia."

EMBARRASSMENTS

"... as the entire company kneeled looking at me..."

I was performing with Eleanor D'Antuono in the mazurka section of *Etude* choreographed by Harold Lander, when she started to slip and bump into my legs. I went flying off, while she plopped to the floor. For my final pose, I landed on her head. I actually sat on her crown, and the audience started to laugh. When I tried to stand up, I realized that the crown was attached to my crotch. I went down to my hands, as the entire company kneeled looking at me, and the audience became hysterical. In this crazy position, I had to walk -- or, rather, limp -- off stage.

That was the funniest thing that happened to me in my career, but not the most embarrassing. That was at the première of John Neumeier's ballet *The Fairy's Kiss* at the State Theatre in New York.

John had originally created this work for a tall boy and a small girl, but with Cynthia Gregory and I playing the roles, the dimensions were reversed. In the beginning of the pas de deux, there is a very uncomfortable lift. Cynthia's Swiss peasant-style costume was made of a slippery polyester fabric with lots of skirts. The slippery fabric caused her to slide out of my grip so that I almost dropped her.

Luckily, my thumb caught under her shoulder. "Oh wonderful," I thought. "At least she is not down on the floor. But what now?" I could not lift her. My thumb was not strong enough.

This all happened in a split second. I got her high enough to charge with her, like a bull, all the way to the other side of the stage and into the wings.

With a moan I lowered her to her feet.

"Where are we?" I whispered, desperately.

"I have no idea," Cynthia said.

I heard a door slam...hard. John Neumeier had stalked out of the theatre by the stage door.

OVERBOOKED

"'Don't be stupid,' I said ...'Let's get out of here!'"

I was once invited to perform with Natalia Makarova in Atlanta. Overbooked at the time I didn't wish to accept the offer. I doubled my guest- engagement fee, hoping to get out of the situation gracefully, expecting to be turned down. But no luck. They granted my request.

We were performing the *Don Quixote* variations, when a man came out with a bouquet of flowers after the first pas de deux. Natasha looked horrified. Cut the performance short? No. But I smiled at her and said, "We don't have to do the variations and coda."

Natasha held the flowers for one second and then handed them back to the man, who was still standing there.

The audience applauded and the curtain came down.

Natasha wanted to go on and finish the ballet.

"Don't be stupid," I said, personally grateful for the chance to finish early. "Let's get out of here."

But my efforts failed. She insisted on completing the performance.

It was a great success.

LESLIE WOODIES, a former Boston Ballet company soloist, toured the United States and Europe with Dennis Wayne's Dancers. She played Cassie in the international and national touring companies of *A Chorus Line* and appeared recently at the Sahara Hotel in Las Vegas. Ms. Woodies appeared on Broadway in George Abbott's Tony Award winning revival of *On Your Toes*, where in addition to her own roles she was second cover for Natalia Makarova and first cover for Dina Merrill. In 1988, she had the pleasure of joining the reunion tour of *On Your Toes* in Los Angeles and San Francisco. Other credits include the films *Echoes* and *A Chorus Line*, Principal Player in a New England Telephone commercial, the "I Love New York" industrials for United Airlines and Coca-Cola, and principal role in the pre-Broadway try-out of *Drumwright* with John Cullum.

Leslie Woodies

TAKE FIVE

"By the time I was halfway through the dance, smoke was rapidly filling the theatre."

I was playing Cassie in a touring company of *A Chorus Line* in Tulsa, Oklahoma, in the summer of 1981. The house was packed, and the show was going well. We came to the halfway point at which Zach gives everyone a five minute break, and calls out to me to stay on stage to perform the solo *Music and the Mirror*.

The other dancers left the stage. I walked down center stage. But there was an unsettling, distracting feeling in the air. I began to hear a strange murmuring rise from the audience.

I couldn't figure out what was happening. I remember thinking -- Do they hate me? Is my skirt falling off? Is there something going on behind me? What?! The rumble got louder and louder. And then, still dancing, I noticed that the air in the spotlights was cloudy.

By the time I was halfway through the dance, smoke was rapidly filling the theatre, and some of the audience was leaving. Scott Pearson, who was playing Zach, called to me: "Cassie -- Cassie -- Cassie!! We're going to stop this audition, and will everyone calmly leave the auditorium. We may have a fire in the building." Someone threw a coat over my shoulders and we all went outside.

That audience deserved a commendation! There was no panic, and instead of going home, they waited patiently until they learned that the fire was really up the street. The wind had pushed smoke into the air shafts of the theatre.

Blowers were turned on, and the air soon cleared. The audience all came back in, and we picked up the show where Zach gives everybody five. Just as before, everyone else on the stage left, Zach asked me to stay, and I walked down center stage.

The first line of the scene is, "Well, this audition is really interesting, isn't it?" It brought the house down! It was the perfect release. We all chuckled and went on to finish the show.

TORN CURTAIN

"My focus was on stage right ...when I heard a long, loud rip."

I was in a revival of *On Your Toes* at the Kennedy Center in Washington, D.C., in December, 1983. The show was directed by George Abbott, with the original choreography by George Balanchine, and additions by Peter Martins, and Donald Saddler. Natalia Makarova, who played Vera Baronova, headed the splendid cast.

In the beginning of Act II, there was a scene (later cut) on a bare stage. To get into this scene, a stage door set was rolled off-stage left, while an outside-the-theatre drop was raised. On several occasions, the drop caught on the stage door and started to tear.

On this particular night, I was in place for the scene change. The lights came up. The scene started. Our focus was on stage right, on Vera and Sergei, when I heard a long, loud rip. It was the weight of the pipe, as it ripped the drop in two and came crashing to the floor. We stood in frozen horror as they brought the curtain down. The heavy pipe had hit not one of us -- but Natasha!

That great lady suffered a concussion and a broken shoulder. But she returned three months later to open with us on Broadway -- and to win the Tony Award.

Natalia Makarova

OFF TARGET

"I was feeling very temperamental one evening, as happens sometimes."

I was in the revival of *On Your Toes* on Broadway in 1984. In an early scene, I am in a bedroom, as Vera Baronova, reading in a newspaper gossip column that my lover, Morrosine, has been at El Morocco with some redheaded, big-boobed floozy. I become hysterical. Anuska, the maid, is cleaning up and I turn to her and say, "And shoes! I ask for a decent pair of shoes." (Of course, there are fifty pair of shoes lying around everywhere in the room.) "You don't care how I look," I yell. "You don't care if I go out barefoot!" I then throw a shoe at her.

The shoe was supposed to hit the door just when Dina Merrill, playing Peggy Porterfield, entered. Well, I was feeling very temperamental one evening, as happens sometimes, and my aim was off. Instead of hitting the door, the shoe hit a vase that was sitting on a podium next to the door. It broke with a huge crash. Then, because the vase had been filled with crystal marbles to weigh it down, that noise was followed by another one: the drumming of all those marbles bouncing across the stage -- blump, blump, blump.

The audience, of course, began to laugh. Dina's first line was, "Darling, what's troubling you?" She tried to say it, but started to laugh and could hardly speak. I did my best to continue the dialogue, but by now the marbles were bouncing and rolling all over the place, and I was starting to laugh too. I couldn't stop.

At that point, George S. Irving entered playing Sergei. He was supposed to stumble over the shoe, but instead he slipped on the rolling marbles and almost fell on his butt. We were all laughing so hard that we stopped the show for about five -- or maybe even ten -- minutes.

A nonbreakable vase was brought in for the rest of the performances.

PATRICIA MCBRIDE began studying ballet in her home town, Teaneck, New Jersey. At fourteen, she was taken into the corps of the New York City Ballet. George Balanchine choreographed a solo role especially for her in *The Figure in the Carpet*. Numerous roles were later created for her. She danced the role of Swanilda in *Coppelia* staged by Mr. Balanchine and Alexandra Danilova, in *Dances at a Gathering* by Jerome Robbins and in *Valse Triste* and *Tea Rose* choreographed by Peter Martins for the New York City Ballet's spring 1988 American Music Festival. She became a soloist in l960, and a principal dancer in l961. Ms. McBride danced in a nationally televised performance at the White House for President and Mrs Carter, and has also been featured on *Dance in America -- Live from Lincoln Center*. In l980, she was honored with a Dance Magazine Award . Ms. McBride retired from New York City Ballet in 1989.

Photo by: Martha Swope

Patricia McBride

MISHAPS

"Anthony slipped. There was a huge tearing sound -- loud enough to be heard from the audience."

I used to love to watch every ballet I could from the wings. I once saw one of my idols, the fantastic Melissa Hayden, performing in *Stars and Stripes* with Helgi Tomasson, when the strap of her tutu snapped while she was making her entrance for a pas de deux. She never missed a step, and gracefully held up her costume by the broken strap from start to finish. It was unbelievable!

As with all dancers, I've had mishaps of my own, of course. One came at the New York State Theatre, as my partner Anthony Blum and I made our exit after our first pas de deux in Jerome Robbins' *Dances at a Gathering*. Anthony was to pick me up, turn me upside down, and exit carrying me into the wing. Since the wing was black, there was usually someone there waiting to help us off. Not this time.

Unable to see anything, Anthony slipped. There was a huge tearing sound -- loud enough to be heard from the audience. The entire back of my beautiful, pink-chiffon costume had been torn to pieces.

I had to make an entrance on the other side of the stage with two other girls, and the wardrobe mistresses were forced to run after me backstage, making what repairs they could, on the run, in order to make me look at least decent. When I made my entrance, the entire costume was held together with pins.

The funniest disaster I ever saw was a New York City Ballet performance of Lew Christensen's ballet *Con Amore*, with Violette Verdy. Once again, I was watching from the wings.

Con Amore was intended to be a humorous ballet, but it was never as humorous as that night. Everything went wrong from the time the curtain went up to the end. The ballet employs many props, and none of them seemed to work. Swords broke, the jewelry wouldn't fasten, a cape was dropped. Part of the scenery came down and landed on Suki Schorer, catching on to her headpiece. One blooper after another, until, fittingly, at the very end of the ballet, the entire set fell over.

Everyone -- dancers and audience alike -- rocked with laughter. It was such a fun ballet that all the mishaps enhanced it, making it that much more ridiculous. But, no matter how hard anyone tried, they could never repeat that performance.

Photo by : Herbert Migdoll

GERALD ARPINO, born in 1928, is co-founder and artistic director of the Joffrey Ballet with Robert Joffrey since 1956. He served as its associate director until he was appointed to succeed Robert Joffrey upon Mr. Joffrey's death in 1988. He was a leading dancer for eight years with the Joffrey Ballet and choreographer of many ballets for the Joffrey including *Viva Vivaldi*, *Trinity*, and for other occasions such as *Birthday Variations*. Mr. Arpino also has had wide experience in Broadway musicals and television. He was given a Dance Magazine Award in 1974 and bestowed an honorary degree of Doctor of Humanities by Wagner College, Staten Island in 1980. Other awards include the 1984 Bravo Award from the San Antonio Performing Arts Association and the 1987 Distinguished Achievement Award from the National Organization of Italian-American Women.

Gerald Arpino

"When the time came to step up before a gracious and smiling Princess Margaret, I was nervous, but ready."

THE KING'S ENGLISH

I was to meet Princess Margaret! The occasion was "Dance for Dance," a black tie benefit performance, the Contemporary Dance Foundation Gala, held at the Hotel Pierre in New York City, on October 27, 1977.

The Princess would be the Patroness of the event, certain to be a memorable evening. The "Pierre" is one of New York's most distinguished hotels, and several of America's leading dance companies were to perform in its elegant ballroom. My own work, *Touch Me*, would be performed by Christian Holder.

I was very excited by the chance to greet the Princess, but I was also somewhat daunted by the prospect of actually speaking to her. As with many Americans, I found myself a bit self-conscious as to how I would sound to someone from the upper reaches of British society. I knew that the English prided themselves on their speech patterns and their precise use of the language. It was, after all, the King's English -- and the Princess was literally a member of the King's family!

Being a performer, I rehearsed. I selected the exact words I would use to address the Princess, and carefully practised my pronunciation.

When the time came to step up before a gracious and smiling Princess Margaret, I was nervous, but ready. I bowed properly, and proceeded to enunciate as clearly and distinctly as I could,

"I - am - pleased - to - meet - you - Your - Royal - Highness."

"How d'ja' do?" responded the Princess.

VIOLETTE VERDY, became in 1977 the first woman ever to be appointed artistic director of the Paris Opera Ballet serving until 1980. Born in Brittany, France, Ms. Verdy received her ballet training in Paris. Her first professional engagement was with Roland Petit's Ballets des Champs Elyssés de Paris. In 1957, she joined the American Ballet Theatre, where she created the title role in Birgit Cullberg's *Miss Julie*. Ms. Verdy later joined the New York City Ballet, for which she danced twenty-five principal roles. George Balanchine created roles for her in several ballets: *Liebeslieder Walzer*, *Episodes*, *Jewels*, *La Source*, *Pulcinella*, etc. In 1983, she served as artistic director of the Boston Ballet. The following year, she returned to the New York City Ballet as a teaching associate. Ms. Verdy has received many awards including a Dance Magazine Award, 1968, Chevalier de l'Ordre des Arts et Lettres, 1971 and others. "Ballerina", a biography of Ms. Verdy written by Victoria Huckenpahler, was published in 1976.

Photo by: Shonna Veleska

Violette Verdy

TEST OF NERVES

"I never imagined something like this would ever happen to me."

One of the first ballets I performed after I joined American Ballet Theatre in 1957 was *Strings*, by John Taras. John is a wonderful choreographer, and *Strings* was his first important ballet, and a beautiful piece at that.

During a performance of *Strings* at the Greek Theatre in Los Angeles, I went completely blank. I stopped in the middle of the stage. I never imagined something like this would ever happen to me. I rehearsed a lot and was always prepared. But I was tired and nervous because I wanted to do especially well.

The action around me was fast and furious; I realized that I was going to be in the way, so I quickly left the stage. The wings were filled with dancers, amongst them Erik Bruhn. Knowing very well what was happening, Erik took me by the shoulders. "You've got to go back," he said.

"But Erik," I said, "I don't remember anything."

"Just quiet down and collect yourself," he advised me, "and it will all come back."

It was a test of my nerves. All of sudden my feeling of desperation disappeared and all the steps started to come back to me. I quickly joined the rest of the dancers and found myself again center stage.

For me, it had been a fierce challenge to overcome this unexpected blank-out. Thanks to the wonderful help of my friend, Erik Bruhn, the audience didn't have time to notice any problems -- only the dancers knew.

42

FERNANDO BUJONES, born in Miami, Florida in 1955, received his first ballet training in Cuba. He entered the School of American Ballet at the age of twelve, and three years later made his professional debut partnering Gelsey Kirkland with the André Eglevsky Ballet. At the age of nineteen, he joined American Ballet Theatre, becoming the youngest principal dancer with any ballet company at that time. Mr. Bujones was the first American dancer to win a gold medal at the International Ballet Competition at Varna, Bulgaria, in 1974. In the same year, he also received a Dance Magazine Award. Now, Mr. Bujones is a freelance artist based in Brazil, making guest appearances around the world. Kultur, Inc. distributes a video tape with Mr. Bujones demonstrating classical male variations.

Photo by: Zeida Cecilia Mendez

Fernando Bujones

EARLY MORNING PERFORMANCE

"All I can remember is doing grand jetés down fifteen flights of stairs."

I was performing with Natalia Makarova at the Edinburgh Festival in July 1977, as James in *La Sylphide*. After my second performance, I went to the hotel for the night and went to sleep.

At 3:00 a.m. a fire alarm rang.

All I can remember after that is doing grand jetés down fifteen flights of stairs in my pajamas, only to find when I reached the lobby that the fire had been put out.

I felt as exhilarated as if I had just finished dancing my variation all over again, and the stage curtain was being brought down.

LUIGI was born in Steubenville, Ohio, in 1925. He started singing at age five in local amateur contests. At age thirteen, Luigi worked in cabarets, dance halls, and night clubs before becoming a classical dancer. Once discovered by Gene Kelly, a talent scout for Metro-Goldwyn Mayer, he got a role in the film *Annie Get Your Gun*, originally shot with Judy Garland. He worked with many famous choreographers, dancers and directors including Gene Kelly, Fred Astaire, Danny Kaye, Leslie Caron, Bing Crosby and others. After a crippling automobile accident, he created for his own rehabilitation the Luigi technique which is taught in college dance departments and studios around the world. Luigi has trained thousands of dancers and actors and gives seminars in such faraway places as South Africa, Japan and Germany. In 1988, he was honored in Roma, Milano and Torino.

ACCIDENT

"Only my determination and my love for dance helped me walk again."

A tragic automobile accident left me unconscious for ten days. Even after I woke up, my eyes were totally crossed and my face was paralyzed. But on the inside, I kept dancing all the time. I never stopped. That was the only thing that kept me alive.

Only my determination and love for dance helped me to walk again. After my seventh operation, I was released from the hospital. My eyes were still bad, and I had double vision. But I wanted desperately to dance again.

The American Ballet Theatre was holding an audition. Lucia Chase was the director and Eddie Canten was ballet master. Lucia had liked me before my accident, so I talked myself into going to the audition.

I had always been a good jumper, and my leaps and beats were fantastic. But at the end of the audition, the boys had to pirouette à la seconde turn and and pull-in for a double turn and land on their knee.

I'm not sure exactly what happened, but after I got to my knee, I heard Lucia's voice in the distance. "My God," she exclaimed. "I thought he could dance!"

My career as a classical dancer had come to an end.

CONFESSION

" 'But Mother,' I protested. 'If I go to confession before the ceremony, there will be no ceremony.' "

I went home for my brother's wedding.

The night before the wedding my mother said, "You must go to Holy Communion with us in the morning."

"I can't," I explained. "I didn't go to confession, and now it's too late. It's almost midnight."

"You can go to confession before the ceremony," she insisted.

"But Mother," I protested. "If I go to confession before the ceremony, there will be no ceremony. I have not been to confession in twenty-five years!"

"It's all right," my mother assured me with a convincing smile. "All you have to say is, 'Bless me, Father, for I have sinned. I am in show business. That's all.'"

NORBERT VESAK, internationally acclaimed choreographer, dancer, teacher and stage director, was born in Vancouver, British Columbia, Canada. He was trained in Merce Cunningham, Martha Graham and the Luigi dance technique, among others. He had served as artistic director of several organizations before assuming that role for the New World Ballet (a company specially created for the New World Festival of the Arts), Miami, Florida, in 1982. Mr. Vesak performed with many companies, a soloist modern dancer with his own company, Norbert Vesak and Dancers, and an actor with Playhouse Theatre Co. etc. His versatility is apparent in much of his prolific choreography since 1960. Mr. Vesak has choreographed *Belong*, *The Ecstasy of Rita Joe*, *Samson and Delilah*, *The Merry Widow*, *The Rite of Spring* and many more. He continues a very busy schedule as a guest choreographer all over the world. For his choreography, he received two gold medal in 1980, one in Varna, Bulgaria, the other in Osaka, Japan.

Norbert Vesak

A HEART THAT BEATS IN 3/4 TIME

"In my last visit to see 'Papa' Shawn ... we had a wonderful afternoon recalling the good (and trying) times we had spent together."

I was very fortunate to be one of the last private students of Ted Shawn, "The Father of the American Dance." My first teacher, Josephine Slater, had been a student of his in the late 1930s and early 1940s. "Jo" was one of the few dancers still teaching Mr. Shawn's method of dance in the late 1950's, when I came to her as a neophyte. It was logical that I would go to study at Jacob's Pillow, established by Ted Shawn in the 1930s in Becket, Massachusetts, as headquarters for his Men Dancers, and I did, from 1960-64, first as a scholarship student and later as production assistant to John Christian. My very close friendship with Ted Shawn endured until his death. He often said that I was his first "grandchild" (though I would not have dared call him "Grandpa" Shawn).

In my last visit to see "Papa" Shawn, shortly before he died, I travelled to Jacob's Pillow with my creative associate designer, Robert-Glay De La Rose, and we had a wonderful afternoon recalling the good (and trying) times we had spent together. As we were about to leave, "Papa" Shawn said to me, "Remember, Norbert, I always said that my heart beats in 3/4 time? Well, now I even walk in 3/4 time!"

And with that, he stood up to leave the room. Putting one hand on his chair, and then moving first one foot, then the other, he said, "You see? Chair-two-three/ Table-two-three/ Doorway-two-three/ Banister-two-three --"

These are my last memories of Ted Shawn, a man I loved dearly, -- using the furniture to help him walk in 3/4 time.

Many years later, I happened to see Ms. Katherine Hepburn in the play *West Side Waltz* at the Curran Theatre in San Francisco. There in the final scene was Ms. Hepburn, using a walker and moving -- Walker-two-three/ Walker- two-three/ Walker-two-three -- and saying, "You see! Now I even walk in waltz time!"

The incident brought tears to my eyes, it was so true to the memory I had of "Papa" Shawn. When I went back stage to tell the story to Ms. Hepburn, she was moved to know that her portrayal was so right. So correct!

"Oh," she said, "what a lovely bit of history of the American arts you have just shared with me!"

Photo by: Anne Kirchbach

Photo by: Constantine

LOTTE GOSLAR, born in Dresden, Germany, has a unique mixture of theatre, dance and pantomime, entirely her own creation. In 1943, she joined Hollywood's celebrated Turnabout Theatre. Ms. Goslar is the director, choreographer and costume designer of the Pantomime Circus. She has created many editions for her Circus, formed in 1954, and made many transcontinental tours. She choreographed the dances *Die Fledermaus, Babar the Elephant, Charivari* a clown's ballet for the Joffrey Ballet, and many others. She also did the film sequences for Marilyn Monroe, her friend and pupil. Furthermore, Lotte Goslar Pantomime Circus was on a Columbia Broadcasting System half hour feature special.

Lotte Goslar

SUCCESS

"How sweet it is -- "

Success, how sweet it is -- applause, good reviews, friends coming backstage to tell you you've never been better, strangers saying, "Where have you been all my life?" In spite of the fact that you know full well it could not have been all that good -- how sweet it is!

The biggest applause I ever got came in Chicago, where I performed with the great actors George Voskovic and Jan Werich (refugees like myself) in a special program for their Czechoslovakian compatriots. I had danced some years before in their fabulous Liberated Theatre in Prague, and now I was to join them again on that special evening, performing some solo pieces. I had just finished my first number, a short curtain-raiser, when an avalanche of applause broke loose such as I had never experienced before. Not three curtain calls, not five, not ten, but at least fifteen!

At that time, I always took my bows in character, and pretty soon I was out of fresh ideas. I could not see the audience because the spotlights were shining directly, blindingly into my eyes. Finally I went as far to the front of the stage as possible to get a look at this extraordinary crowd. And I saw that they had all risen to their feet and were standing with their backs toward me. What had happened: Eduard Benes, the Czech President-in-exile, their great hero, had arrived and was standing in the balcony. And I had taken my bows -- in character!! --toward their behinds. The only one who had seen me making a fool of myself was Benes. I hope.

HELGI TOMASSON, born in Reykjavik, Iceland, where he began his ballet training at the National Theatre, went to Copenhagen, Denmark, at the age of fifteen to study and perform at the tiny Pantomime Theatre at Tivoli Gardens. While on tour with his Ballet U.S.A., Jerome Robbins offered Helgi a scholarship at the New York School of American Ballet. He was seventeen then, in the fall of 1959. Later, Helgi joined the Joffrey and the Harkness Ballet, becoming a most celebrated dancer. Representing America, he received the Silver Medal in 1969, at the Moscow International Ballet Competition. A year later he was invited to join the New York City Ballet as a principal dancer. He has been the artistic director for the San Francisco Ballet since 1985. He has choreographed *Theme and Variations, Polonaise, Op. 65* (to the music of Mauro Guiliani), *Ballet d'Isoline, Contradances* and *Menuetto* (Mozart), which was created for the New York City Ballet and premiered in their 1984 summer season at the Saratoga Performing Arts Center. His most recent ballets include *Valse* and *Beads of Memory.*

Helgi Tomasson

KABUL

"The theatre was newly built ... and we discovered to our horror that there was no heating system in the building."

I first came to America in 1960, and joined the Joffrey Ballet Company two years later. In 1963, one of our tours took us to Kabul, Afghanistan where we were to perform on behalf of the United States State Department.

It was February, and when we arrived there was snow on the ground and it was very, very cold. I was very excited, since our cultures are so different. The city was fascinating, and, seemingly, a hundred years behind the times.

I found it amusing to see people walking around barefoot in the snow, while their heads and necks were covered. Our interpreters explained to us that the Afghans believe that when their necks are warm, their entire bodies will also be warm. Coming from Iceland, I believe the opposite. When your feet are warm, so will be your entire body.

The theatre was newly built by the Russians. We discovered to our horror that there was no heating system in the building. It was so frigid that when the stage crew rolled out the dance floor, it cracked. As far as I can remember, we couldn't even use it.

Before the performance, our bodies were so frozen it was impossible to warm up. For the first time in my life, my toes were so cold they were numb. Kerosene lamps were placed around the wings, but the only thing we got from that was a very bad smell.

The ballet for that evening was one of Alvin Ailey's, in which the boys are bare-chested, which did not help any of us at all. Mr. Joffrey talked to us before the curtain went up: "Try not to hurt yourselves," he said. "Do whatever you can within the limitation of the choreography."

The curtain went up, and we saw the audience bundled up in fur coats. We tried to do our best, watching our own breath on stage before us. Eventually, we realized that the audience was in love with what they had seen. But their applause could not be heard, because they were wearing gloves and mittens.

I can laugh about it when I look back now, but at that time, it was a cold day in Kabul.

56

MELISSA HAYDEN, born in Canada, a solidly schooled classical dancer, has been teaching, coaching and staging a variety of George Balanchine's ballets all over the world, since 1973. She was principal dancer with the New York City Ballet, 1949-73. She worked with Boris Volkoff and his Canadian Ballet until she moved to New York, where she danced with the Radio City Music Hall. For two and half years, Ms. Hayden danced with the American Ballet Theatre until 1948 when she went on a South American tour organized by the Cuban ballerina Alicia Alonso. Then in 1950, she returned to New York for the 1949-50 season of George Balanchine's new company, where she had major roles in *Apollo*, *Serenade*, *Ivesiana*, *Concerto Barocco*, *The Four Temperaments*, *Symphony in C*, etc. Practically every great American choreographer worked with Ms. Hayden. She became internationally known as she made guest appearances with companies and played the role as the ballerina in Charlie Chaplin's *Limelight*, and as the Sugar Plum Fairy in a German film version of *The Nutcracker.*

Melissa Hayden

BECOMING A BALANCHINE BALLERINA

"One by one, the other dancers left, and there I was -- still waiting. I kept looking at the clock. It seemed like an eternity had crowded itself into a few minutes of time."

My mother introduced ballet lessons to me when I was twelve years old. At that time, I enjoyed swimming and playing the piano. I never dreamt that I would become one of Balanchine's ballerinas.

Eventually, I joined the Canadian Ballet, where my teacher Boris Volkoff was director. Years later, I decided to make the move to New York. My first engagement there was with the corps de ballet of the Radio City Music Hall, where I managed to squeeze in ballet classes in between rehearsals and performances.

Shortly thereafter, I joined American Ballet Theatre. There, I had my first opportunity to work with Mr. Balanchine, in the spring of 1948, when he was invited to choreograph *Theme and Variations* for a production at the Metropolitan Opera House. He also choreographed some of the pieces on tour, and would often rehearse the dancers.

Because ballet is young in this country, many dance companies are financially unstable. They had particularly little patronage in the 40s and 50s , and the seasons were short. Our company was furloughed early in the spring, leaving many of us out of work. A friend asked me to join a Broadway show, which was something many classical dancers did at that time. I hesitated at first, but finally accepted out of necessity.

I appeared in two Broadway shows that summer, leaving the second one with three weeks to go in October, 1948, to join Alicia Alonso's newly formed company for six weeks in Cuba. I was a success and stayed with the company for a year, travelling with them throughout South America.

Meanwhile, back in New York, Mr. Balanchine was beginning to recruit an increasing number of dancers for the New York City Ballet who had not been trained in his school. Nicholas Magallanes, a long-time friend of mine who had joined Alicia's company in Cuba, left to join Mr. Balanchine. Shortly after, I received a cable from Mr. Balanchine inviting me to join the New York City Ballet.

Naturally I was thrilled by his offer, and even more excited when I received an airline ticket for New York. I was in awe of Mr. Balanchine. Everyone knew he was one of the great ballet choreographers of the 20th century.

Once in New York, I could hardly wait to get to the studio to take class. My eagerness to see Mr. Balanchine again, and to have him welcome me to his company, grew into nervous tension as the class went on. But it came to an end without Mr. Balanchine even once entering the classroom!

One by one, the other dancers left, and there I was, still waiting. I kept looking at the clock. My life history passed before my mind's eye. I was twenty-seven years old. My training had been in Canada. I'd had two years with the American Ballet Theatre, and one very successful one with Alicia Alonso. I had worked with many great American choreographers, and now here I was -- invited to become a Balanchine dancer!

Suddenly, he was there in the doorway, looking into the room!

I hurried over to greet him. But he looked right past me, as if he was looking for someone else. Then, he turned and moved away. I heard his footsteps fading down the hall.

I felt crushed. Devastated. *He did not even remember who I was.* Why had he sent for me? Perhaps Nicholas had talked to him about me, and about my success with Alicia Alonso. I decided to find out for myself. I picked up my dance bag and made my way to the office. There I met the secretary, who gave me my schedule and explained, with a reassuring smile, that indeed Mr. Balanchine expected me at his 9 a.m. rehearsal.

It was an unpromising beginning to a beautiful future.

REALITY

"That little piece of netting seemed to get longer and heavier by the second, as my imagination ran wild..."

Sometimes what happens on stage, and in the minds of the dancers, wildly differs from the illusion we work so hard to create. An example of this occurred once while Jacques d'Amboise and I were tyring to perform magic in the German version of *The Nutcracker*.

Jacques and I shared a successful partnership, and did many guest performances with other companies. Our costumes in the piece were covered with jewels, and our variation was filled with pirouettes, and stunning, but difficult lifts.

Suddenly, a piece of net from my tutu became entangled on a pearl in Jacques' jacket. Freed almost immediately, the tutu was ripped in the process, and the torn netting set my mind racing.

There was some time left before the finish of the pas de deux, and that little piece of netting seemed to get longer and heavier by the second, as my imagination ran wild, driven by every note of the enchanting music. With so many pirouettes, I worried, there was a good chance that my prince charming's hands could get caught in the dangling netting -- not to mention my feet. Fear started running though my body.

The audience seemed spellbound. But surely, I felt, they must have noticed that something was troubling me.

But then, suddenly, we were in the finishing pose. The audience's applause swept away my fears, and every problem seemed to melt with that final bow.

In the wings, I was greeted with a smile -- and a pair of scissors.

MIKHAIL BARYSHNIKOV, born in Riga, Latvia, studied at the Vaganova School under the great teacher Alexander Pushkin. At eighteen, he entered the Kirov Ballet as a soloist, making his debut a week later, in the peasant pas de deux in *Giselle*. That same year, he won the Gold Medal at the First International Ballet Competition in Moscow. After the Kirov, he was a principal dancer with both the American Ballet Theatre (1974-78) and the New York City Ballet (1978- 79), and made guest appearances with the Martha Graham Dance Company and many other international dance companies. On Dec 1, 1980, Mr. Baryshnikov became artistic director of the American Ballet Theatre and served until 1990. He was nominated for an Academy Award for his role in the film *The Turning Point* and an Emmy for *Baryshnikov on Broadway* in 1979. Furthermore, he starred in the feature film *White Nights*, has been the subject of several books, and has made many appearances on television, including "Dance In America", "Live From Lincoln Center", and "Alive From Off Center". In 1989, he enjoyed great success on Broadway in the leading role of *Metamorphosis*.

Photo by: Anne Marie Heinrich

JOAN EHEMANN STONE, born in Chicago, was trained at the Stone-Camryn School of Ballet in Chicago by Bentley Stone and Walter Camryn and joined the Ruth Page Ballet Company at the age of fifteen. Upon graduation from high school, she joined Leonard Sillman's Broadway hit, *New Faces of 1952*, later working under Richard Rogers, Oscar Hammerstein II, in the long-running musical, *Carousel*. Ms. Stone was a member of the American Ballet Theatre, the Chicago Lyric Opera, and the New York City Opera. She appeared as a soloist in television productions choreographed by Agnes de Mille, and in the film *Boy on a Dolphin* (20th Century Fox) and for the Columbia and Public Broadcasting Companies. She was the ballet mistress for Sybil Shearer Company. Ms. Stone has been active for years in promoting dance in Chicago, heading organizations, lecturing and guest teaching.

Joan Ehemann Stone

AN IMPROVISED PAS DE DEUX

"There was only me ... and Igor Youskevitch!"

In 1956, the American Ballet Theatre performed *Helen of Troy* at the San Francisco War Memorial Auditorium. I was cast in the secondary role of the lead lamb of Paris, the shepherd who kidnaps Helen.

The legendary Igor Youskevitch played Paris.

During the Prologue, the scrim, which was supposed to rise on the first scene, stuck. Instead of a stage full of dancers, there was only me, a lowly lamb -- and Igor Youskevitch!

Forced to abandon the choreography, we improvised a pas de deux.

What a great moment for me!

GABRIELA KOMLEVA received a People's Artist of the U.S.S.R. award, a Russian Federation Prize, and the Varna International Competition Prize for 1966. Prima ballerina of the Kirov Theatre in Leningrad, she studied with the best teachers her native Soviet Union had to offer, including the distinguished V. Kostrovitskaya. Not only did she perform the classics, such as *La Bayadère*, *Sleeping Beauty*, *Giselle*, etc., but also Ms. Komleva danced in the *Crystal Palace* by George Balanchine, *The Moor's Pavane* by Jose Limon, in Roland Petit's *Miniatures* and *Pas de Quatre* by Anton Dolin. She took an active part in the creation of modern ballets; for example, I. Belsky created especially for Ms. Komleva the part of the girl who lost her beloved in *The Shore of Hope*. Ms. Komleva, author and choreographer, often performs on Soviet television. After graduating with highest honors from the Choreographer's Department of Leningrad Conservatory, she has been running the refresher class at the Kirov Theatre.

Gabriela Komleva

ENCOUNTERS WITH KARSAVINA

"And suddenly there I was, standing in front of an armchair where a very
plump grey-haired lady was sitting majestically. So this was Karsavina!"

The name of Tamara Karsavina -- the legendary ballerina of the early 20th
century, who first won fame at the St. Petersburg Maryinski Theatre and then world-
wide renown through her work in the Diaghilev Ballet Company -- was for a long
time but a remote and glorious piece of history for me.

Like Karsavina I was born and lived in Leningrad (formerly St. Petersburg), I
graduated from the same ballet school in Rossy Street (formerly Theatre Street); I
plodded through to the fine points of ballet in the same classrooms. Also like her, I
first danced on the stage of the small School Theatre, and then on the famous stage of
the Maryinski (now Kirov) Theatre. I saw Karsavina's photos, and listened with great
interest to the tales about her, but I never imagined that she herself would enter into
my life, and more than once. The fact that those contacts were fleeting and infre-
quent only makes them more distinctly alive in my memory, and so much the dearer
to me.

Karsavina was remembered in our theatre. To my teachers, she was very
much a real and vital presence. My first husband's father, Boris Shavrov, a well
known dancer and fine actor in bygone days, would often talk about her. At that time,
Shavrov had already abandoned his dancing career and worked as a coach at the
Kirov Theatre. He pronounced the very name "Tatochka" with veneration and gentle-
ness.

He asserted that all the boys (the senior pupils of the Theatre School) were in
love with her. He, too, along with his classmates, languished when meeting their
favorite, who, naturally, never suspected this boyish epidemic. And, like them, he
used to spy through the slightly opened door of the famous rehearsal hall while Karsavina was rehearsing and working at the barre. The most courageous youngsters
managed to go on "spying" at the theatre. These daredevils soon had exciting news to
tell their more timid friends. In the intervals between the curtain calls, having finished
her bows, Karsavina and her partner, Petr Vladimirov, secluded themselves in the narrow space between the curtain and the stage portal (called in our theatre the "iron
box") and -- they kissed there! The news was whispered from one boy to another, and
it remained a part of the school's life for a long time.

In my imagination, Karsavina remained as she was in these stories: a charming brunette, accustomed to admiration, a bit flighty, and, of course, very young. So

my acquaintance with her was all the more unexpected. It happened in London during the guest tour of the Kirov Theatre in 1966. There was a reception in the bar of Covent Garden in honor of the publication of Anton Dolin's book "The Sleeping Ballerina", which was dedicated to another famous Russian ballerina, Olga Spessivtseva.

The whole of London's artistic community seemed to be there, and we were invited, too. At that time, I already knew Mr. Dolin from our mutual work in Canada: during our guest tour there he had taught us his *Pas de Quatre*. When he saw me, he smiled and, after complimenting me on my London performances, took my hand and began to lead me somewhere.

While walking, he explained: "After having seen you in The Leningrad Symphony Karsavina declared that she liked you very much and insisted that you be introduced to her."

And suddenly there I was, standing in front of an armchair where a very plump grey-haired lady was sitting majestically. So this was Karsavina!

I was introduced to her. The old lady spoke in the very deep voice of a heavy smoker: "You are quite a boarding-school girl in everyday life," she said. "But your dancing was quite different: strong, convincing, grand."

And suddenly her eyes glittered naughtily, and I recognized in this quite elderly lady the other one, full of charm and youth, whom my imagination had been drawing for me.

A few days later a copy of the book about Spessivtseva was delivered to me. It was Karsavina who had sent me this book, with a moving inscription in it. And a little bit later she presented me her own book, "Theatre Street", with her autograph, which was not yet issued in the Soviet Union at that time.

Years later, a review written by A. Agustin in the Spanish newspaper *Ultima Ora* compared me to Karsavina. I was very pleased to find myself thus related to the best traditions of the Russian ballet, which had been incarnated in the splendid art of Tamara Karsavina.

In the following years, as my English friends who visited Tamara Karsavina told me, she often asked about me and the parts I was dancing. These friends of mine were passionate ballet lovers, and not infrequently they flew from London to Leningrad to see performances of the Kirov Company. Then, back at home, they would share their impressions with Karsavina. Through them, Karsavina learned about my Nikiia and asked for some photos. She examined them very attentively, nodded approvingly, and saying, "It's so. It's true. Everything was like that ... so they have preserved everything!" She asked our common friends to convey to my teachers and to me her words of gratitude for keeping Petipa's great creation, *La Bayadère*, alive.

At last the remarkable occasion approached: the 23rd of January, 1977 -- the centenary of my favorite ballet, *La Bayadère*. Before that anniversary performance I worried a lot, as I prepared to dance the part of Nikiia. Again and again, I read the memoirs of Yekaterina Vazem, for whom this ballet had first been staged, about her work with Petipa.

And suddenly -- an unexpected present! A message of greeting from Tamara Karsavina! "It gives me great pleasure," the great ballerina wrote, "to send my greetings on the occasion of the jubilee performance of *Bayaderka*. This was one of my favorite ballets in our repertoire, and one in which I often performed on this stage. For me, this ballet also has poignant memories, for it was in *Bayaderka* that I danced in this theatre for the very last time and so it pleases me to be with you in spirit on this historic occasion, knowing that this unique ballet and the great traditions of our school are being faithfully preserved in this, the fondly remembered city of my birth."

These cordial words, and the special attention of Karsavina, imparted assurance and strength to me. When on stage I felt confident, and fully able to enjoy the genial choreography. When I danced in a video of *La Bayadère*, in 1979, I often recalled Karsavina and tried to imagine how she would have danced in this ballet. But Karsavina could never see the film, for she had died one year before its release.

Then, in 1983 -- the 200th anniversary of the Kirov Theatre -- there was a jubilee exposition in Bakhruchin Central Theatre Museum in Moscow. Among many other exhibits, there were materials connected with Karsavina. And there among them was her greeting, so memorable to me, on the occasion of the centenary of *La Bayadère*.

WILLIAM REILLY was trained at the Stone-Camryn School of Ballet in Chicago. He was a premier danseur with the Netherland Ballet, and ballet master and lead dancer with Jerome Robbins' *Ballet U.S.A.* He choreographed and danced in a number of Broadway shows. He was a lead dancer in *My Fair Lady* by Lerner-Lowe and *I Can Get It For You Wholesale* by David Merrick. Currently on the faculty of Marquette University Dance Department, Mr. Reilly also serves as the choreographer for the Florentine Opera and the Milwaukee Symphony's Kinder Concerts, and directs his own Academy of Ballet in Milwaukee. In 1989, Mr. Reilly, together with Shirley Reilly, his wife, appeared as the dance team Vincent and Vanessa in Steven Sondheim's production of the Broadway musical *Follies* at the Chicago Light Dinner Theatre.

William Reilly

WEEKEND PASS

"The three gorgeous showgirls wined us, and dined us, and even drove us back to the camp ..."

Before I joined the Army, I danced at the Biltmore Hotel in Los Angeles. In those days, the Biltmore's dining room offered variety shows, with star singers, comedians, and many, many showgirls. I, as the token male, danced in front of the girls in the big production numbers.

Later, when I was in the Army, I was one of the soldiers sent to take part in an atomic test at Camp Desert Rock, Nevada. While there, we were given a weekend pass to Las Vegas. I arrived in Las Vegas with some of my buddies, and we did the rounds. We were all in the lobby of one of the casinos, dressed in our baggy soldiers' uniforms, when I heard someone call my name.

I turned around to see three gorgeous six-foot tall showgirls come running toward me across the lobby. They all swept me off my feet, showering me with kisses. My soldier buddies almost passed out with shock.

The girls, of course, were showgirls I'd danced with back at the Biltmore, who were now working in Las Vegas. They wined us, and dined us, and even drove us back to the camp in one of their convertibles.

We made quite a sight. Three G.I.s, pulling up to the camp gate in a big convertible, with three knockout showgirls hugging and kissing us. Word spread throughout the camp, and from then on I was everybody's buddy.

Photo by: Lynn Krause

ADAM PERNELL, born in 1952, is one of the most sought ballet accompanists in New York City and throughout the country. After winning several prestigious musical competitions in his native Philadelphia, he entered Temple University in 1970 on a full musical and academic scholarship. Upon arriving in New York in 1975, he began playing modern classics for former Martha Graham dancer, Denise Jefferson at New York University. He then went on to play for American Ballet Theatre, the Joffrey Ballet, Dance Theatre of Harlem, Maggie Black and David Howard. He has worked with such dancers as Martine van Hamel, Kevin McKenzie, Rudolph Nureyev, Natalia Makarova and Mikhail Baryshnikov. He also played for Gelsey Kirkland during her coaching sessions with Stanley Williams. In 1987 and 1988, Mr. Pernell was the only pianist to work with Dame Margot Fonteyn during her series of master classes in New York City. He has written several ballet scores for former Joffrey ballerina, Trinette Singleton and in collaboration with former Ballet Russe de Monte Carlo dancer, Dorothy Lister. Mr. Pernell has produced a very successful record, <u>Great Operatic Selections for the Ballet</u>.

Adam Pernell

ORIGINALITY

"Maggie Black always liked to have opera music played in class."

Since I began working as a ballet accompanist, I've been very privileged to associate with many great artists. Some of the most interesting moments of my work have come from watching dancers react to my music. Some ignore it, others just use it as a way of keeping time, and still others seem to embody it and be inspired by it.

Working with New York teacher Maggie Black, I will always remember seeing how the ballerina Martine van Hamel would not just dance to the music, but, in her words, always try to "interpret the music." What a revelation she was.

Maggie Black always liked to have opera music played in class. One day she told me that it was her teacher's idea (the incomparable choreographer, Antony Tudor) to use opera in class to help the students with their phrasing, and to encourage them to create a more expansive style.

Later that day, at the American Ballet Theatre, I saw Mr. Tudor in the elevator. I jokingly told him that I had stolen an original idea of his. Before I could finish, he smiled with that glimmer in his eye and said, "My dear young man, I've never had an original idea in my life!" And this coming from a man who created a completely new way of using the ballet vocabulary!

Photo by: Hannes Kilian

PIERRE WYSS, born in 1957, in Lausanne, Switzerland is the artistic director and choreographer of the Ulm Ballet Theatre in Ulm, West Germany. He received his training at the Royal Academy of Dancing in London with Alicia Markova, and in his native Switzerland, in Paris, and at the Stuttgart Ballet School in West Germany with Anne Wooliams and Alex Ursuliak. He won the Swiss National Competition Award in 1974 and the 1975 International Dance Competition Award. He has choreographed many works, such as *Firebird Variation*, *Slavic Dances* and *Serenade for 13*. He has performed as guest artist with both the Royal Ballet and the Stuttgart Ballet.

Pierre Wyss

TRAINING

"The next morning, I could hardly get out of bed."

It wasn't until about two years after I'd essentially retired from being a dancer that I finally got proof of how important it really is to train every single day of your career.

In the two years since I'd stopped dancing with the Stuttgart Ballet, I had been creating ballets for them, and was beginning to become established as a professional choreographer. No one in Basel, Washington, Ulm -- or even in my home company of Stuttgart -- thought of me as a dancer anymore. In my normal routine, I would rarely even step into the studio until after the daily training session was already over.

I had just left Stuttgart and moved to Ulm, where I was preparing to take over the artistic direction of the Ulm Ballet, when a desperate phone call came from Marcia Haydee in Stuttgart. The Stuttgart Ballet was about to leave for a five-day tour to Brussels, and she needed me to jump in and replace someone in Maurice Béjart's *Gaité Parisienne*. I would have to be in Stuttgart that same evening, in order to leave with the company for Brussels.

I made it, rehearsed on the train, went on, and danced the part -- all without too many problems. But the next morning, my muscles were so cramped that I could hardly get out of bed. I was so stiff from dancing without the usual daily training that I literally had to crawl down to the breakfast room of our hotel.

Things deteriorated a little later, back in Ulm. I had just gotten rid of the pain from the Brussels performances, when a dancer with the Ulm Ballet broke his foot the day before the première of our *Coppélia*. Nobody could be found to replace him, so there I was again, jumping in. But for three acts this time!

Fortunately, I had seen some rehearsals, so I had an idea of the steps -- steps that included such charming little tricks as double tours, pirouettes, and *grands fouettés*. I don't know where in heaven I found enough technique to pull it off, but I did the dress rehearsal and the premiere.

I felt quite awful about my performance, but the dancers around me, whom I was to direct and choreograph the next season, told me I had been excellent. And, although I had shaved my beard off in an attempt to remain incognito on the stage, some people in the audience recognized me and were very excited about my dancing. I was very happy to hear all that, of course. But I was very unhappy for the next few weeks, suffering from muscle cramps and other goodies of that sort. All dancers should stop for a couple of years and then have to jump in to dance a part or two -- then they would know the real necessity of training.

Photo by: V. Sladon

MARIA YOUSKEVITCH, a native New Yorker, was trained by her parents, Anna Scarpova and the legendary Igor Youskevitch. She toured the United States as a member of their Ballet Romanique Concert Group, and has appeared as a guest artist on many ballet specials on television, as well as in a full-length motion picture version of *Giselle*, filmed in Madrid. Ms. Youkevitch was a soloist with the American Ballet Theatre and the Maryland Ballet, was ballet mistress for the Ballet Metropolitan in Columbus, Ohio, and served as principal coach and instructor for the New York International Ballet Competition in 1984 and 1987. She travelled around the United States, setting classical ballets including *Giselle*, *Coppélia*, *La Fille Mal Gardée* and *Romeo and Juliet* for regional companies.

Maria Youskevitch

COSTUME TROUBLES

"As soon as my toes touched the floor, however, I realized that I could not go any further. I was stuck there on Romeo's back."

Perhaps one of the worst moments of my performing career came while on tour with my father's company, Ballet Romanique. We were the first ballet company to perform in the new Civic Theatre in San Diego, and I was dancing Juliet in a one act ballet that my father had choreographed from the Tchaikovsky's *Romeo and Juliet Overture*.

It was opening night and everything was going well until we got to the bedroom pas de deux. After a beautiful arabesque, I ran to Ralph Robinson who was dancing Romeo. He lifted me under my arms and swung me around to his back. Once there, completely off the floor and facing the audience, I was to slide down his back to the floor and then bend backward for a kiss. That, at least, was how it was supposed to happen.

As soon as my toes barely touched the floor, however, I realized that I could not go any further. The pearls on the front of my costume had gotten caught on the zipper on back of Ralph's jacket. I was stuck there on Romeo's back. I wriggled this way and that, trying to free myself, but no matter how I squirmed, I could not move. Seconds became eternity. I was starting to panic when my puzzled partner asked, "What's the matter?"

"I can't move," I replied. "I am stuck."

The music kept playing while I strained and tugged at my costume. I finally broke free, but only at the expense of ripping my costume, which turned out to be harder to do than I thought, and then praying that I would still have some cover left. By that time, I had stopped listening to the music altogether, and I had no idea what was coming next. I looked desperately at Ralph. "Attitude and turn left," he prompted me calmly. Suddenly my concentration came back, and we went on to finish not only the pas de deux but the whole ballet flawlessly.

The headline of the review in the next day's paper read: "Mishap Mars Opening of *Romeo and Juliet*." True to form -- and despite the fact that the rest of the evening had gone so beautifully -- all the press could think of was disaster.

I once had another kind of costume problem while dancing in Leonide Massine's *Gaité Parisienne* with American Ballet Theatre at the State Theatre at Lincoln Center. I was one of the Cocodettes as well as dancing in the famous cancan. Once the Cocodettes enter with the Billiard Players, they remain onstage for almost the entire ballet, except for the famous pas de deux, which was first performed by Alexandra Danilova and Frederic Franklin. This meant that those of us who were both Cocodettes and cancan dancers had only the time taken by the short pas de deux to carry out a major costume change.

There was no time for us to go back to the dressing rooms, so we changed right in the wings. Three or four other girls helped each of us to make her change. It was like a drill. One girl unbuttoned your Cocodette costume, took it off, and helped you slip into your cancan costume. While she was doing you up, another girl helped you off with your tights and on with your garter, while two other girls (one for each leg) helped you off with your shoes, on with your stockings, and then back on with your shoes again, each of them buckling a single shoe.

It was a carefully choreographed but frantically performed routine. And, even while all this was going on, to me and around me, I was busily fixing my hair and changing my headpiece.

One night in the middle of all this madhouse activity, I suddenly realized that I had forgotten to pre-set the red flower that I needed to wear on my head during the cancan. It was still up in the dressing room!

"Oh, my God!" I thought. "I'm going to be the only girl without a flower in my hair!" All the girls wore a flower that matched the color of their ruffles and the panties underneath their skirts, and since my costume was red and gold, I needed a red flower. Without one, I would not only stick out, I would surely be reprimanded later.

There was no time for anyone to go to the dressing room to get it. In a panic I looked around backstage for something I might possibly use as a substitute. With the seconds ticking rapidly away, I spotted a pile of paper napkins some of the stage hands must have left behind after a hurried lunch. I couldn't believe my eyes. *They were red*!

I grabbed one, opened it up, pinched it in the middle, and then frayed the edges a little to make them look more like soft petals.

"How does it look?" I kept asking the girls nervously. "Does it look sort of like a flower? Is it going to pass?"

I had more than its appearance to worry about. It was difficult to bobby pin the napkin to my hair and make it stand up at the same time. I didn't know if it was going to stay up there without a net or hook to secure it in place. Having it fly off during the dance would attract more attention than not having it at all. But it *was* red -- and I needed red. With the pas de deux music nearing completion, I decided to risk it.

The orchestra began the introduction to the cancan. Everyone was yelling desperately for me to get in place for my entrance. I ran to the wings and kept right on running out onto the stage, making it in the very nick of time.

Luckily, my napkin-flower stayed in place. No one even noticed the difference. But, all through the dance, I was silently thanking the crew for eating in a restaurant that used red napkins, and for leaving them around backstage!

JAMES MOORE, an alumnus of the Stone-Camryn School of Ballet in Chicago, was ballet master with the American Ballet Theatre and artistic director of the Royal Swedish Ballet, before accepting a teaching position as professor of dance in 1975 with the University of Wisconsin, Stevens Point. Mr. Moore was a member of Jerome Robbins Ballets U.S.A. troupe in 1958. He was an assistant on the ballet *Les Noces*, choreographed by Mr. Robbins in 1965, and has since restaged the work for both the Royal Swedish Ballet and the Hamburg Opera Ballet in West Germany. Mr. Moore was a judge for the International Ballet Competition in Varna, Bulgaria in 1977. He assisted Mr. Robbins on the award-winning *Jerome Robbins on Broadway*.

James Moore

SHOES

"During one performance I neglected to switch shoes during the first fast change --"

Am I the only one who has this problem with shoes?

The first Broadway show I danced in was *Seventeen*, back in 1951 at the Broadhurst Theatre. I had three very quick, but complete, costume changes in the first act. They involved a brown suit, a blue suit, and a "sporty" suit, and thus, three pairs of shoes -- one black, one white, and one brown -- to go with them. The shoes were laid out in sequence to help me make the countdown, but during one performance I neglected to switch shoes during the first fast change. As a result, I ended up in the wrong color shoes for the next three scenes.

At intermission, a very unhappy director appeared backstage, irate about the young dancer who stood out from the rest because of his shoes. (And here I thought I stood out because of my dancing.)

In 1959, I appeared with Jerome Robbins' *Ballets U.S.A.* at the Alvin Theatre. In one of the ballets, called *Opus Jazz*, we each wore a brightly colored top -- with shoes to match -- for the first three movements. Then, after a quick costume change, the lights came up for the fourth and final movement revealing us all in pure white.

The first phase of this last movement ended with a slow bow. One evening as I completed this bow, my downcast eyes came to focus on a pair of extremely bright purple sneakers!

Raising my head, I saw Mr. Robbins standing only a few feet away in the wing. He was not smiling.

Photo by: Kirk Fleischauer

CYNTHIA HARVEY, born in San Rafael, California, received her ballet training in California at the Novato School of Ballet with Christine Walton, and later became a member of the Marin Civic Ballet. She joined the American Ballet Theatre in 1974 and became a principal dancer in 1982. Roles created for Ms. Harvey include Gamzatti in Natalia Makarova's *La Bayadère* and the Fairy Godmother in Mikhail Baryshnikov's production of *Cinderella*. Her varied repertoire includes the sweetheart and mother in *Billy the Kid*, the pas de trois from the *Guards of Amager*, Juliet in *Romeo and Juliet*, Odette/Odile in *Swan Lake*, etc. In 1986, Ms. Harvey joined the Royal Ballet as a principal dancer -- the first American ballerina to be made a member of the company. There, she created two roles: the Moon in Wayne Eagling's *Beauty and the Beast*, and the Woman in David Bintley's *Still Life* at the Penguin Café. With the Royal Ballet, Ms. Harvey had various roles in the *Firebird*, Princess Aurora in *Sleeping Beauty*, the leading role in Jerome Robbins' *Opus 19/Dreamer*, etc. She has also appeared as a guest artist with several ballet companies.

Ted Kivitt

AN EARLY PERFORMANCE AT THE KENNEDY CENTER

"I thought surely they would close the curtains -- but they didn't!"

One of the most unusual experiences I ever had was at the Kennedy Center in Washington. I was with the American Ballet Theatre at that time, and it was one of the very first performances to open the Center.

We were dancing *Etudes* that night choreographed by Harold Lander. I was waiting in the wings for my entrance when a swag curtain weighted down with 25-pound canvas bags of lead pellets was opened. The bags must have gotten caught on something, because they suddenly ripped open and all of the pellets poured out onto the stage.

The stage lights had not yet come on. The first indication I had that something had happened was a strange noise that came from the stage area. It sounded as if a driving rain was suddenly washing over the stage. When the lights came up, I was horrified to see what looked like millions of beebees rolling toward the footlights. I thought surely they would close the curtain -- but they didn't

I made my way downstage to start my pirouettes, moving as cautiously as I could. Seconds later, the light system blew out and I found myself isolated in total blackness. I couldn't even see my hand in front of my face.

Some flashlights appeared in the wings, and I was straining my eyes to see, when I heard a loud voice from the wings saying, "Ted, come off stage. Come off stage!" And then, at almost the same time, but from the other side, a voice was shouting, "Ted, stay on. Stay on!" At that point, I didn't know what to do, so after waiting for awhile I left the stage.

The lights eventually came on again, I got back into position. The audience applauded and the conductor raised his baton to pick up the music where we'd left off. I started on my first couple of steps -- and the lights blew out again!

The audience moaned.

Again from the wings I heard someone telling me, "Ted, stay on stage," and from the other side a different voice telling me come off.

By this time I was furious, but I stayed on awhile longer before carefully making my way off stage again in total blackness. Just as I got to the wings, the lights came on again, but there were still literally thousands of beebees to contend with.

I don't know how I ever got through the next section because there were so many turns from second position, attitude turns, and first arabesques. In this dangerous situation, four girls in point shoes were trying to dance behind me, and their shoes were filled with these tiny lead pellets.

When I finally finished the section, I was ready to scream. The stage manager said they would close the curtains and sweep the stage floor. Then while the stage was being swept the lights blew out again! And all we could see were those big brooms, bumping into one another, not accomplishing a thing -- just pushing these little beebees around.

Finally the lights came on again, and this time they stayed on. But despite all the efforts to sweep them up, the beebees had taken over the stage.

It was a miracle no one was hurt.

MARIA CALEGARI, born in Bayside, Queens, became a member of the New York City Ballet at seventeen, then a soloist in 1981 and a principal dancer in 1983. Among the works she performed for the New York City Ballet, were principal parts in George Balanchine's *Agon*, *Apollo*, *Bugaku*, *The Nutcracker*, (as both the Dewdrop and Sugar Plum Fairy), *Western Symphony* and *Who Cares*. She is equally well represented in Jerome Robbins' *Afternoon of a Faun*, *The Cage*, *Concertino*, etc. and originated roles in Mr. Robbins' *Antique Epigraphs*, *Eight Lines* and others. Her repertory includes several ballets by Peter Martins: *Rossini Quartets* and *Piano-rag-music*. During the New York City Ballet's 1988 American Music Festival, she originated roles in Bart Cook's *Into the Hopper* and Jean-Pierre Bonnefoux's *Five*.

Photo by: Martha Swope

Maria Calegari

BECOMING A BALLERINA

"My mother and I found ourselves in an elevator with George Balanchine. What a strange man, I thought."

One always arrives at the New York City Ballet with great expectations, great hopes and dreams that one yearns to come true. I've been lucky enough to have realized those dreams, and to have become a part of that world, and yet I can still remember when the ballet and its people were strange and exotic to me.

I can remember, for example, a time when I was only fourteen and my mother and I found ourselves in an elevator with George Balanchine. We had just seen a wonderful performance of *Firebird* at the New York State Theatre, Lincoln Center.

Mr. Balanchine eyed me up and down, and I him. What a strange man, I thought -- and all because he was wearing a silk scarf around his neck instead of a tie! I didn't know that in the years to come I would not only work for and dance for this strange man, but secure from him both my most basic and most inspired dancing techniques.

Mr. Balanchine was a very funny man. Working so much with young dancers, he was well versed in dealing with stage mothers as well. Although I never had a stage mother in the nasty sense of that term, he liked to pretend I did. I remember a beautiful day in Saratoga Springs, at the Avenue of the Pines, where the company was gathered for photographs to be taken for <u>Vogue</u> magazine.

Some members of the company were up in arms about having to walk up a very long road and up a very steep hill to get into position for the pictures. For myself, I was simply overwhelmed just to find myself opposite Mr. Balanchine in his yellow Mercedes. As we arranged ourselves for the photos, I heard his voice. "Maria, dear," he said humorously. "Please move so that your mother will see you."

I realized that I had half hidden myself between my partner and the nearest pine tree. I thought I would die from embarassment at the time, but it was by just such little nudges as this that Mr. Balanchine helped bring me out of myself to become the ballerina I am today.

By the time I joined the New York City Ballet at the age of seventeen, I had already performed in several of Mr. Balanchine's works as a student at the School of American Ballet. In one of them, called *Serenade*, I played the role of the Arabesque Girl, or Dark Angel, so named because she is the portent of fate for the man in the ballet.

When I was nineteen, Mr. Balanchine allowed me to dance the role at the New York City Ballet. It was a wonderful role, and I will never lose the awe I felt at being part of this great work with this fine company. It was an integral part of my early training as a ballerina. And as we worked on it, he kept nudging me to come out of myself.

At one rehearsal, Mr. Balanchine was unhappy with the way I was embracing my partner. It was in the last movement, the "Elegy," in which I was one of three women, all out for the same man. In the end, he is mine. This was very nice, but Mr. Balanchine wanted me to know it -- and to *show* it.

"Please," he said. "Can you be a little bit more like one of Charlie's Angels from California?" He was referring to the stars of the popular television show of that day about three very beautiful, exciting and sexy women detectives. I saw what he meant. Pretty soon the embrace became more of what he wanted and needed to see!

At another rehearsal, he asked about my long red hair which I had been wearing tucked on the top of my head. "Dear, have you cut your hair short for your boyfriend?" he joked. "Or is it still long?"

Well, I immediately took down my hair, and from then on the "Elegy" was always done with all three of the ballerinas' hair worn down and flowing.

NILO TOLEDO formed a Centre of Fine Arts in Seminole Country, Florida. He was a dancer, teacher, choreographer, performer and a jazz adjudicator for the Canadian Dance Festival in 1975. He performed on Broadway in *West Side Story*, *A Funny Thing Happened on the Way to the Forum*, and *Irma La Deuce*. He choreographed the play *Cross and Sword* for Florida State University . Mr. Toledo also directed two record albums for Stepping Tones Records (Al Gilbert), <u>Jazz Jazz Jazz</u> and <u>You Can Do It with Nilo</u>. His performing group, The Nilo Toledo Concert Dancers, have appeared throughout Florida and Georgia.

Nilo Toledo

COMEDY ACT

"The audience started laughing ... I couldn't figure out what was so funny."

One summer, while I was on tour with Danny Hoctor's Dance Caravan, I inadvertantly turned a very serious blues number into a comedy act.

I was right in the middle of the number when the audience started laughing. Since the number was such a serious one, and it seemed to me to be going quite well, I couldn't figure out what was so funny. Not until I caught a glimpse of a piece of light blue material in a place it didn't belong.

My costume was a dark blue jumpsuit with a light blue shirt underneath. The jumpsuit had a zipper that ran from the crotch all the way up the front. But now, both I and the audience could see a light blue area appearing down by the crotch. I realized that the zipper was slowly separating from the bottom up. As I kept dancing, the steadily growing opening revealed first the ends of the shirt, then the dance belt --

But I kept dancing. At the end of the number, I grabbed Danny Hoctor's microphone. "That" -- I told the audience, to a burst of laughter and applause -- "you have to pay for!"

Photo by: Henry Leon

HAMBURGERS

"One day, Goldie and I took the bus into Baltimore."

Back in the mid-'60s, I was just beginning my dance career. I met Goldie Hawn when we both worked in the outdoor drama, *The Common Glory*, in Williamsburg, Virginia, and we became close friends.

Only 20 years old, and never having been north of Florida before, I found it difficult making my way in the dance world. Fortunately, Goldie and my other friends convinced me not to return to Florida. The arts were not exactly booming there at that time.

I auditioned for Frederic Franklin at the National Ballet School in Washington, D.C., and won a scholarship to go there. Soon after, Goldie and I both got into the Maryland Civic Ballet Company, which was under the direction of Igor Yousekvitch. It was based near Washington, in Baltimore. One day we took the bus together into Baltimore.

We were both starving to death when we arrived, and, as we walked to the theatre, I spotted a big building with a huge sign that announced, "Hamburgers." I quickly suggested to Goldie that we stop and get one before going on to the rehearsal.

Goldie broke into her wonderful, soon-to-be-famous giggle. When I asked her what was so funny about two hungry dancers stopping for hamburgers, she stopped laughing long enough to explain. "Nilo, honey, here in Baltimore, Hamburgers is a big department store!"

So much for eating.

TO SLEEP, PERCHANCE TO SNORE

"I thought to myself, 'If I don't close my eyes, at least for a few minutes, I'm never going to make it....'"

I had left my home in Florida to teach at a weekend convention. On my return, I got delayed in a distant airport. The next plane back would not leave until morning. Although I was tired out from the convention, and people were stretched out all around me on the floor, I forced myself to stay awake all night. I was scheduled to teach a class in Florida in the morning, and I was determined not to miss my flight.

Once the plane set down in Florida, I rushed for class. I made it, but, by then, I was thoroughly exhausted.

Even as the class began, I thought to myself, "If I don't close my eyes, at least for a few minutes, I'm never going to make it through the day."

I decided to start the class with a muscle-relaxing exercise in concentration. I had everyone (including me!) lie down on the floor. Then I spoke soothingly to the class, telling them to erase all thoughts and other distractions from their minds: everything except for the sound of my voice.

All at once I sprang to my feet jolted with the electricity of fear. My embarassment was so comic that the exercise in relaxation turned into hysteria.

I'd been so exhausted that the sound of my own voice had put me into a deep sleep, only to be awakened by my own snoring!

FRANK HATCHETT began his dance training at the age of eleven in East Hartford, Connecticut. The Frank Hatchett School of Dance was started at the Dunbar Community College in Springfield, Massachusetts. In 1982 in New York City he set up the Hines and Hatchett Studio, which was renamed the Broadway Dance Center in 1984. Mr. Hatchett teaches jazz for many leading dance organizations around the country, and created a popular *Jazz Dance Video for Dancers, Instructors, and Choreographers.*

Frank Hatchett

VALUABLE LESSONS

"Is this the way it all ends? Is this how I'm going to end up?"

I set out to be a professional dancer as soon as I could get out of school. I was working at the Dunes Hotel in Las Vegas when a well dressed gentleman came up to me one night after the show. He lavished me with flattering compliments. He told me that I really stood out on the stage, and how electric my performance had been. I was the youngest member of the cast, and all this praise made me feel just great.

The man went on to say how much I reminded him of himself in his younger days. He too had been a dancer, he explained. He'd performed in films, as well as in concerts and stage shows all over the world. He'd even danced for royalty.

He finished our conversation by telling me to always look out for my financial security, to save my money, and to look ahead. I thanked him sincerely and went to my dressing room.

I was wandering through the hotel the next day when I came to the kitchen area. Without really knowing why, I stopped there, as if held by some strange power. I was looking around the kitchen with no particular purpose when I suddenly recognized a familiar face. It was the well dressed man who had praised me so highly the night before. He was a dishwasher in the hotel!

At first I was in shock: depressed. "Is this the way it all ends?" I thought. "Is this how I'm going to end up?"

Then I took his advice as what it was -- a very valuable lesson. I never renewed my contract at the Dunes. I went home to go back to school and finish my education in business administration.

Indirectly, my experiences in Las Vegas were helpful to my future in another way as well. I was back home in Springfield, Illinois, staying with my grandmother, when I decided to walk over to a friend's house and show him my collection of photographs of all the stars I'd met in Las Vegas.

I was walking along the street when I saw four kids trying to break into a neighborhood store. Something about them must have gotten to me. Instead of calling the police I decided to go over and talk to them. Fortunately, they didn't get rough or anything when I walked up to them and asked why they were trying to break into the store -- they just got scared.

When I asked them if they could dance, their fear turned to surprise. "Oh, yeah," they said. "We can dance." They told me they had a singing group, and showed me some street stuff they did. In return, I showed them the book of photographs from Las Vegas. They were really impressed. I told them that if they wanted to come over to my grandmother's house I'd show them some dance steps they could use in their singing group.

They were skeptical at first, but they came anyway. I showed them some steps, and after a while everybody relaxed. They even asked if they could come back sometime. "Sure!" I said.

Well, they came back the next day, and they brought some friends along with them. And the day after that, they brought more friends, until it became a regular thing where all these kids came over to my grandmother's after school. Finally, my grandmother put her foot down. "Wait a minute," she said. "This has got to stop!"

I rented a small store front with the money I'd saved from my Las Vegas performances and started regular classes. We even formed a group called The Entertainers. Pretty soon, all the kids were bringing their little brothers and sisters for classes, and the Frank Hatchett School of Dance was born.

POOR BUNNY

"But one night ... someone shouted, 'The comedian's sick, so they cut his act!' There was immediate panic."

I was playing an African Prince in the big production number of a show called *Small Affairs* in Chicago. The number was called "Rhythm of the Drums," It was about a New York socialite who goes on safari and falls in love with a young Prince in the jungle. The Prince, however, is under the watch of a powerful jungle Queen. The number was essentially a power play between the two women. The Prince spent most of his time on top of a huge jungle drum, while the socialite dances seductively, trying to entice him to come down to her.

"Rhythm of the Drums" came right after the first act in the show, which was a comedian's routine. His final applause was the cue to get into position for our dance number. While he was on, we'd all sit around backstage in costume playing cards until it was time to go on. I always wore a bathrobe over my costume, and a pair of huge fuzzy slippers my grandmother had given me. I loved those slippers because they were so warm. I'd wear them all the way to the wings, then slip them off and leave them there, where they'd be waiting for me when I came offstage to keep my feet warm all the way back to the dressing room.

But one night we were sitting around playing cards when someone shouted, "The comedian's sick, so they cut his act!" There was panic. Everyone dashed to the stage to get in place for the big dance number.

The drums started. The curtain opened. I had made it. I was in place kneeling on my drum. Then it dawned on me -- I was *still* wearing my fuzzy bunny slippers!

I started swaying back and forth, picking up the rhythm of the drums. Using the swaying motion to cover what I was doing, I kicked the first of the slippers off my foot. It flew toward the back of the stage. No one seemed to notice. This was going to work. Feeling relieved, I kicked off the other slipper ...

Perfect timing. The slipper sailed smack into the body of a dancer who was just making his entrance with a grand leap! It bounced off him and landed right in the middle of the stage. There it sat, a huge fuzzy bunny crouching in the middle of the jungle. It took all the concentration the dancers could muster to keep from bursting out laughing as the bunny slipper was kicked around the stage like a soccer ball for the rest of the scene.

As for me, I just knelt there on my drum, looking princely regal, as if it had nothing at all to do with me.

Barbara Remington

CAKEWALK

"I would play with the audience -- bourrée-ing and flirting with them like a stripteaser."

I danced the part of Venus in the tongue-and-cheek ballet *Cakewalk* with the Joffrey Ballet Company. My costume was a lavender, one-piece, satin leotard with lots of ruffles around the legs, and a big skirt that came off for my solo.

I was supposed to come on stage with a big balloon, attended by three ladies and a male dancer with a large cape. The cape hid me until, like a magician, he would sweep away the cape revealing me and my balloon. I would dance, moving the balloon in front of one part of my body to another bourrée- ing, flirting with the audience, like a stripteaser -- always concealing some part of my body with the huge balloon.

But one night in New Orleans, while I waited to go on and the stagehands inflated that big balloon, I heard a loud bang. When the music started, I had to go out there under the lights, in front of the audience, with no balloon.

I gave the audience the show of my life. I danced the entire solo just as it was choreographed. I did exactly what I would have done with the balloon, moving my hands and arms as though I were holding it in front of me.

Thunderous applause! Apparently the audience had no idea I should have been carrying a balloon.

Afterwards some of the dancers said, "Leave it like that. Forget the balloon." But, from that time on, Robert Joffrey always insisted we keep an extra balloon backstage. Just in case.

GABRIELLA TAUB-DARVASH, born in Rumania, received a scholarship from the Rumanian government to study ballet at the Kirov Ballet School in Leningrad. She majored in choreography and drama at the University of Performing Arts in Moscow, and graduated in 1957, magna cum laude. As a guest artist and choreographer/teacher Ms. Taub-Darvash has created many ballets in Israel and the United States. She presented *Cinderella* and *Giselle* in 1985 and 1986, respectively, in New York City. In 1976 she founded the Darvash Ballet School in New York which produced the first American female gold medalist in the international competition in Lausanne, Switzerland, in 1980.

Gabriela Taub-Darvash

DIFFERENT DIGITS

"The pianist stopped, and there was an uncomfortable hush in the room."

When I first arrived in the United States, I was offered the position of resident choreographer for the Garden State Ballet in Newark, New Jersey. My English was not very good, but since ballet is a universal language I assumed I wouldn't have too much trouble.

At that time, I didn't know that the English language used different words for fingers and toes. This is not the case in any of the other five languages I already spoke, nor in the two others that I have investigated since. So, in my first class, I told the dancers to stretch their fingers, when I meant that they should point their toes.

There were strange expressions all around the room as the dancers extended their arms and stretched out their fingers, straining more and more as I repeatedly chided them: "No good, no good -- *just stretch your fingers!*"

I noticed that one of my advanced students was trying to get my attention. The pianist stopped and there was an uncomfortable hush in the room. A little nervous, and blushing, the student relaxed her fingers.

"These are fingers, Madame Darvash," she said timidly. "And these," she added, beautifully pointing to her foot, "are toes."

CHARTHEL ARTHUR received her first dance training in Pasadena, California. She auditioned for Robert Joffrey, who offered her a scholarship to the Joffrey Ballet School. After five months of study, she became an apprentice, and, only three months later, she rose to become a member of the Joffrey Ballet Company. She made her professional debut at the first White House Conference on the Arts, and performed at the White House for President Lyndon Johnson. During her thirteen years (1965-78) with the Joffrey, Ms. Arthur appeared in every New York season, and toured throughout the United States and Canada, as well as in the Soviet Union, London, and Vienna. Since 1984, Ms. Arthur has been the artistic director of the "Summerfest" in Grand Rapids, Michigan.

Photo by: Herbert Migdoll

Charthel Arthur

ARM INJURIES

"As I finished the roll over my partner's back, I missed catching his arm and fell --"

I remember being really frightened twice while on the stage. Strangely enough, both times involved arm injuries. The first time came when I was dancing the role of the student in *The Lesson* by Flemming Flint. In the midst of a pas de deux, my partner Edward Verso, who was dancing the ballet master, hit his elbow on a piece of the set. He quietly told me that he was injured and didn't know if he could continue.

I was really scared. The ballet lasts about twenty-five minutes and more than half of it was yet to be performed. During that time Edward and I were scarcely ever off the stage. I couldn't imagine continuing the story without him. The only other dancer in the entire ballet was playing the Pianist, and he was dressed in woolen clothes and character shoes. I didn't see how I could possibly dance for fifteen minutes with him. Or, even worse, alone. Fortunately for everyone, Edward did keep dancing until the end, improvising to avoid doing any lifts.

The other time I was frightened, involved an arm injury of my own, during a performance of Jerome Robbins' *Interplay*. At the very end of the first movement, the girls do a rapidly rolling cartwheel over the backs of the boys as they bend forward. As I finished the roll over my partner's back, I missed catching his arm and fell -- full weight and full steam ahead -- on my right hand.

My elbow, which had been locked straight, was severely jammed. I was sure I had broken my arm, and there were still three movements of the ballet to go. Well, somehow I got through them. And I continued performing throughout the rest of that City Center season. But for about seven months after the injury, I had a nasty case of tennis elbow and could hardly bend my arm.

Photo by: Jack Mitchell

LAURA YOUNG, born in Cohasset, Massachusetts, has been the director of both the Boston Ballet's Summer Dance Program, and Boston Ballet II since 1986. She joined the Boston Ballet in September 1963 and she toured with the company in the People's Republic of China in 1980. Ms. Young retired in 1989. She had a triumphant performance as Odette/Odile with guest star Rudolf Nureyev in the Boston Ballet's London debut of its *Swan Lake* in July 1981. She played leading roles in world premières by the Boston Ballet's Associate Director Bruce Wells including *Prelude* and *La Fille Mal Gardée* and in Bruce Marks' *Pipe Dreams*.

Laura Young

TOURING

"There I was in my white tutu, the vision of Don Quixote's dreams, performing a Nadia Comenici routine."

One of my most treasured experiences came when I was touring the United States with Rudolph Nureyev in *Don Quixote* with the Boston Ballet in 1982. I was dancing Kitri, opposite Rudolph, and in rehearsal I had difficulty holding the last balance in the third act pas de deux, which is executed after a promenade in arabesque penche.

Rudi noticed this, and with his very thick Russian accent he told me: "Laura, you must think of a very hungry dog with his stomach all sucked up."

In that night's performance he sang, "Hungry dog!" at me between his teeth during the penche promenade, when our backs were to the audience. I had to stifle a laugh, doing my best not to let it shake my concentration, but by the time we faced the audience again, I had obediently sucked in my stomach.

It worked. I held the balance until the last breath of the music faded away. As I then stepped forward and passed him for the final pirouette I couldn't help but make a small bark under my breath, just loud enough for him to hear.

We shared a good laugh together, happy in the knowledge that the image he had passed on to me had helped us to give a memorable performance. Since then, I have coached my own students in the hungry-dog theory. When they find out it works, they laugh too.

We toured abroad that same year, beginning in the Far East, performing in the Republic of China, Hong Kong, and Israel for three months, before winding up in Italy and France.

We were performing George Balanchine's *Four Temperaments* in a small town in Italy when I slammed my head into an iron pipe backstage while rushing to get my leg warmers from behind a plywood cyclorama.

I felt my body spin and fall to the floor. Someone saw me and helped me up. I barely heard a voice that seemed to come from a great distance asking, "Are you all right?"

"I don't know," I said.

When I put my hand to my forehead, I could feel a gigantic bump. I must look like a unicorn, I thought.

"Get me to wing two," I said, and someone pointed me in that direction.

As soon as I got on stage, I realized that I was in the wrong place, and the movements seemed faster than ever before. No wonder we call this section the "Bug Dance," I thought, with all its twistings of hips and split second timing. I just kept moving, trying to get myself to the correct spot.

The next section of the ballet involved four couples. I was partnered by David Brown. David was a wonderful partner, and through the entire passage my feet barely touched the ground, but it was a miracle we made it through.

After the performance, our interpreter took me to the local hospital. It was already midnight, and the place looked like a closed deli. Stools were placed upside down on the emergency table, and no doctor was in sight. My interpreter asked that I be given an X-ray to determine if I had a concussion.

"But no one is here," the attendant said.

"Oh," the interpreter responded, "then we'd better return to the hotel."

"No, she can't leave," the attendant insisted, pointing to me. "She must stay here."

"What happens if I stay?" I asked.

"Nothing till morning," she replied. "when the doctor arrives."

I headed for the door. "If she leaves," the attendant protested, accosting the interpreter, "she must sign a paper that we are not responsible if she should die."

I quickly signed the paper and rushed back to the hotel, thinking I'd rather die with friends than with strangers I couldn't even talk to.

An old Roman amphitheatre in Sicily provided a wonderful setting for *Don Quixote*. Unfortunately, the backstage space was very small, so scenery and props had to be shoved wherever there was room.

Near the end of the variations in my first scene as Dulcinea, I realized that a gypsy cart had been pushed diagonally across the wings, blocking my only exit from the stage. I looked around nervously, hoping to spot a hidden exit somewhere. But there was none.

When it was time for me to exit, all I could do was grab the cart and swing myself under it, between the wheels. There I was in my white tutu -- the vision of Don Quixote's dreams -- performing a Nadia Comenici routine.

When it was time for my next entrance, I had to perform my gymnast's routine all over again to get back on the stage. Later I was told by friends that suddenly there was a puff of white net appearing from under the cart -- and then suddenly there I was, bourrée-ing into the bright lights, as if such an entrance were perfectly natural.

Photo by: R.M. Collins III

JANNE JACKSON DEAN, born in 1953 , Geneva, New York, joined the National Ballet of Holland at seventeen, danced solo roles in George Balanchine's *Divertimento No 15*, *Paquita*, and *Sleeping Beauty*. She performed with the American Ballet Theatre from 1976-79, in the movie *The Turning Point*, and in televised productions of *Swan Lake*, *Giselle* and Mikhail Baryshinikov's *Nutcracker*. In 1982 Ms. Dean became a principal dancer with Ballet Oregon, dancing in the *The Nutcracker* pas de deux and in "The Blue Bird" pas de deux from *Sleeping Beauty*. Since 1986, she has been an instructor and co-director of Ballet Dix-Sept at the Central Wisconsin School of Ballet in Wausau.

Janne Jackson Dean

LAUGHTER

"I suddenly saw myself from the audience's point of view and burst into laughter."

I was nineteen and dancing with the National Ballet of Holland. One evening a corps member was sick, and I was asked to dance in the corps -- which I had not done in a long time --in addition to doing my solo part.

Once on stage with the corps, I found myself exactly one musical count behind the rest of the girls. This meant that I was turning out when they were turning in, and vice versa.

I suddenly saw myself from the audience's point of view and burst into laughter. I tried to stop, but my laughter was uncontrollable. Soon the other dancers were laughing too, not even knowing why.

Luckily, I was able to get back on the right beat and the right step, and even to stop laughing. But then -- just when my partner, the late Choo San Goh, had me at the top of a grand jeté lift -- I began to laugh again. With my body shaking from the laughter, I could no longer hold my back properly and Choo San started laughing too. He brought me down so fast that we both almost fell on the floor.

Every time I looked at another dancer, I started laughing all over again, so we all tried not to look at each other until it was finally over. (And what a relief that was.)

On the bus ride home, I received my first negative comment from the director of the National Ballet of Holland, Rudi van Dantzig.

The next day, one of the dancers took me aside. "If it happens again," she said, "just bite the inside of your cheek or tongue -- very hard." That advice has saved me many times since, and I continue to pass it on to my students.

Photo by: Jerry Capps

TIBOR ZANA first danced professionally in his native Hungary, where he was trained in Budapest. In 1961, he received a B.A., and in 1964 a M.F.A. in Television Production and Direction, from the University of Wisconsin in Madison, where he is now a professor. He founded the Wisconsin Ballet Company in 1961. Two ballets with the Birgit Cullberg's Ballet Company, which he produced for television, were shown not only throughout the United States, but in twenty-six foreign countries as well. In 1969, Mr. Zana received the Governor's Award for Excellence.

Tibor Zana

RAW ONIONS

"Then, all of us acting in unison, exhaled towards our partners, just as we'd agreed."

In 1955, I was dancing in the operetta *Count of Luxembourg* at the Operett Szinhaz in Budapest. One of the men had a family still living on the farm. Every spring his parents brought him fresh vegetables, including onions.

Of course, in the theatre there is a rule that we should not eat anything offensive or smelly. But, being pranksters, we men decided one day that all of us would go ahead and eat fresh onions before the operetta's opening waltz. We finished the last bit of onions just before taking our places on the stage.

In the opening waltz, there were two lines of dancers, with twelve girls in one line and twelve men in the other. As the waltz began, the twelve men took two steps towards the girls and extended their arms. Then the twelve girls took two steps towards us and put their hands on ours.

We walked towards the girls. The girls came closer to us. Then, all of us acting in unison, exhaled towards our partners, just as we'd agreed.

Well, this, of course, turned a few heads in the line, and the stage manager caught that right away. And, as we came off the stage, everybody was giggling and howling.

We paid dearly, as we were stripped of three days of pay; but the laughs and the storytelling we got out of that one moment made it all worthwhile.

MARCOS PAREDES, born 1937 in Aguascalientes, Mexico, received a scholarship for the Academia del la Danza Mexicana in Mexico. He was a first soloist with the Ballet de Càmara and Ballet Concierto. Mr. Paredes also danced with the American Ballet Theatre, in the corps, as a soloist and as a principal dancer after 1973. Also known as a costume designer, he has created the costumes for six ballets in the American Ballet Theatre repertory. He retired from American Ballet Theatre and from dancing in 1980. Mr. Paredes restores art for art galleries.

Marcos Paredes

INTERNATIONAL INTRIGUE

"One hears so many stories about the Russians, I began to imagine my toenails being pulled out."

After a successful six week tour, the American Ballet Theatre was due to leave Russia on July 23, 1966. At boarding time, officers stopped each person in line and looked in a book before permitting anyone to climb the boarding ramp to the plane.

When my turn came, I was pushed aside, in a not-too-friendly way. Of course, everyone gave me questioning looks.

The officers let other members of the company pass, but when I tried again, I received the same treatment. "Why?" I asked. At first they would not answer. Finally, one of the officers informed me, through an interpreter, that I could not leave Moscow because they did not have my passport! I had given it to a gentleman at the American embassy some days before, and somehow it had not been passed along to the proper authorities.

I started to feel very nervous. My mind went to New York, before we were to leave for Russia. Gentlemen from the State Department had spoken to the company about what to do and what not to do in Russia. Do not speak to strangers, do not accept gifts -- a long series of "do nots."

I had violated some of those "do nots."

I had, in fact, walked about in the streets, talked to people with the help of gestures and a dictionary, and explored the train stations and the stores. I'd even gone to a hatmaker's shop to have a cap made like the ones the Moscow taxi drivers wore.

But, more importantly, I had some forbidden icons in my luggage -- and even more were secreted in the costume trunks.

Other members of the company and I had purchased the icons from a Mexican friend, studying at the Moscow Conservatory. Certain students at the Conservatory had gone to small towns and bought the icons. They brought them back to my friend to sell. My friend had invited me to the student residence where he lived, and from a closet he presented a suitcase full of the beautiful treasures. I took most of them back to the hotel in my practice bag. It happened that the hotel was locked at 11:00 p.m., and I had to ring the bell for the guard to come and open the door. There I was with the icons poking out of my bag. I hurriedly put my sweater on top, and with a big smile I thanked him, said good night, and hoping he hadn't seen the icons.

Photo by : Kenn Duncan

Immediately I called my friends to come to my room and see them. I offered them for sale, speaking in whispers, in case our chandelier was bugged. Between us, my friends and I bought all of the icons.

Now, at the airport, I started to worry that it had been discovered that I was smuggling art out of the country. One hears so many stories about the Russians. I began to imagine my toenails being pulled out, one by one, until I confessed the whole truth. I wouldn't dance anymore -- and my career was just starting!

I watched the entire company board the plane. I was left at the foot of the boarding ramp, surrounded by officers and interpreters. Then the company's secretary came down the ramp to offer me money. A friend offered to stay, but I told him to go ahead and take care of my luggage. Once they'd all boarded the plane, the boarding ramp was wheeled away.

I watched the row of sad passport portraits wave goodbye, blowing kisses to me. The plane moved onto the runway and then up into the sky.

My luggage with the precious icons was on the plane, and I had only my shoulder bag and a big box with the doll I had bought at the airport. To cover up my nervousness, I turned to the interpreters and said, "Well, which museum shall we go to?" They all laughed.

I was taken into the building, up to the second floor, and into a room set up for a meeting. Around the tables were more men I had never seen before. I was invited to sit. A tall, and heavy-built gentleman rose. Grey haired, perhaps in his sixties, with a very strong and lovely sounding voice, he held a glass of vodka (there were several bottles on the table), and offered a toast in Russian. They were very sorry about what had just happened to me but that there was nothing they could do.

The person next to me translated and explained that the gentleman who had just spoken had been an opera singer. (That explained his voice.) I told them that since the company wouldn't be rehearsing for a few days, there would be no problem if I stayed in Russia. The extra time would let me see more of it. In that friendly mood, we all had vodka, bread, caviar, tea, and mineral water: everything on the table. But, I kept thinking about my toenails being pulled out and which one of these men would be most likely to do it.

We left the room and walked down to the waiting area. A man ran towards me. It was the man from the embassy who had taken my passport. His necktie was undone, and, looking very alarmed, he explained that he had overslept. My passport had been on his night table.

He took me to a ticket window to try to book a flight out, but the lady at the window answered with a dry "nyet!" So he opted for the "treat-them- the-way-they-treat-you" policy and retorted arrogantly. It worked -- she gave me a flight to New York with a stop in Copenhagen.

The man apologized again and left because he was late for work, but I was still skeptical. My plane was announced so I returned to the boarding area and got in line. Again I was stopped and pushed out of line.

This time I was angry, not nervous. I asked the lady who'd stopped me why she did this, and she answered in Russian. I demanded that she speak to me in English. Seeing I was mad, she told me in Spanish that I needed a stamp of "exit" on my passport. I needed it immediately or I would miss the plane.

After more heated words she took me back to the building in a luggage cart. We got the stamp, rushed back, and, finally, I was permitted to enter the plane. I was the last passenger to get on and was barely seated when we started for takeoff.

In New York, the customs clerk was surprised that after six weeks in Russia I had only a shoulder bag, and no luggage. "It is a long story," I told her.

After I was cleared, I went to phone my friend to see if the treasures were safe, but I got no answer. That worried me, because the company should have arrived long before me. Waiting to call again, I heard a man's voice. "Marcos, what are you doing here?" I recognized a friend of one of the dancers. I told him. "Didn't you hear?" he asked. "The plane with the company arrived late in Paris. They missed their connecting flight and had to take a later plane. They'll be arriving soon."

I laughed. When the company's plane was finally announced, I went to the windows overlooking the desks where everyone declared their luggage. I put my elbows on the railing, with my face close to the glass, as though I had a standing room ticket at the opera. The company walked in single file, in the same order they had boarded the plane in Moscow.

As Lucia Chase, our director, approached, she saw me, opened her mouth, and tapped our ballet master, Enrique Martinez, on the shoulder. One-by-one they all tapped each other's shoulders and looked up at me, laughing in surprise. I smiled down with pride and satisfaction and waved to them.

When I returned to the customs desk with my newly arrived luggage, I found the same clerk. "You again?" she said. "Now what?"

"Now," I announced, "I declare my luggage."

"But how come?" she asked.

"I told you," I answered. "It is a long story."

JUDY ANN BASSING is an internationally known choreographer of jazz and tap. She has taught for every major dance organization, several universities, and conducted master classes throughout the United States and Europe. Ms. Bassing was a guest artist at the Joffrey Ballet School, and the New York High School of Performing Arts. She was the recipient of the Los Angeles Drama- Logue award in 1987 for her choreography in *Sugar*, performed at the Lawrence Welk Village Theatre. Ms. Bassing now teaches at the Broadway Dance Center, in New York City.

Judy Ann Bassing

TIP-TAP

"I tell them they must practice this exercise every day, wherever they are ...."

I have a favorite exercise that I have taught to my students all over the world. I call it tip-tap. When I teach them to tip-tap, I tell them they must practice this exercise every day, wherever they are, and whenever they have a few idle moments. I suggest tip-tapping while they stand in line at the bank, talk on the telephone, brush their teeth, wait for the subway, or pause for the light to change on a street corner. When I first teach them the exercise, I tease them and tell them they will be in big trouble if I ever run into them waiting in a line somewhere and they are not practicing their tip-taps.

Well, one of my students was in Switzerland on her honeymoon, and while she was waiting at the Zurich airport she practiced her tip-taps. She was standing there tip-tapping away when she heard a voice behind her saying, "You must be from the United States!"

She turned around and saw a young man standing there. "And you must be studying with Judy Ann Bassing in New York," he continued.

"Yes," she replied in total amazement. "And you must be from the United States, too?"

"No," he answered. "I'm from Yugoslavia. But Judy Ann Bassing choreographs for our jazz company, and when we wanted to do a tap dance number she taught us tip-taps."

So, I guess the tip-taps work all over the world.

Photo by: Frank Marchese

MICHAEL UTHOFF is artistic director of the Hartford Ballet Company. Raised in Santiago, Chile, Mr. Uthoff is the son of Ernst Uthoff who was a soloist with the Jooss Ballet, when Kurt Jooss created such classics as *Green Table* (1932). Michael began his training at the University of Chile. With a grant from the Rockefeller Foundation, he moved to New York to study at the School of American Ballet and at the Martha Graham Studio. He became a member of the José Limon Dance Company in 1964, and later, joined the Joffrey Ballet and the First Chamber Ballet of New York. Mr. Uthoff performed principal roles in works by George Balanchine, Jerome Robbins, Robert Joffrey and others. Since he began choreographing in 1968, he has created more than three dozen dances for various companies, including Joffrey Ballet and the Chilean National Ballet.

Michael Uthoff

IMPROVISATION

"Since nobody was doing anything, I jumped on stage and improvised..."

Right after the Tokyo Olympics in 1965, Gerald Arpino choreographed a ballet called *Olympics.* It was a ballet with a group of men running around, sweating and flexing their muscles. When I danced *Olympics* with the Joffrey Ballet Company, at the City Center in 1967, the lead dancer, Luis Fuentes, fell in the beginning of his variation at the end of the ballet and broke his leg.

There were about three extra minutes left, so two of us decided to run on stage, in character, lift Luis up, and take him off stage. Then, since nobody was doing anything, I jumped on stage and improvised for the next two minutes.

His variation was full of pirouettes and I was not able to turn that well, so I kept jumping from one side to the other, making hand gestures towards the wings that meant another dancer should enter onto the stage. I ran right, then to the left, doing the gestures, hoping somebody would relieve me. Everybody was just standing and staring. No one came to relieve me. Only when a dancer finally came in with a torch could I move again to my own part for the finish of the ballet.

I was pretty exhausted when I walked upstairs, and Mr. Joffrey, who had rushed to see what had happened to Luis Fuentes, looked at me and said: "Did you improvise, Michael?"

"Yes, I did."

"So," he said. "Good."

When I got to my dressing room, I thought to myself, He probably thinks I am the only idiot that would do it.

Probably so!

OUT OF RETIREMENT

"Don't expect me to jump too high...but let's see what we can do."

In 1979, after I had retired from performing, we were on tour to Greenboro, Long Island, with the Hartford Ballet.

We were about to do *Tom Dula*, a work in which I had previously performed the lead role. I was sitting in the audience, and the lights were about to go down, when the manager came over and said: "You know, your lead dancer got hurt and nobody else but you can do it. I think I have a dance belt, that's about it."

I said, "O.K. Is my old costume around?"

The wardrobe mistress rushed to get it ready.

Then I told the stage manager to tell the audience we would be ten minutes late because of technical difficulties.

Fortunately the lead was my former partner, Judy Cosnell. Jean Tears and Robert Buntzen also dancing that night belonged to the original cast. I remember saying to them: "Don't expect me to jump too high, but let's see what we can do."

I got dressed, slapped on some make-up, bent and stretched a little, and in ten minutes I was ready.

It was a dramatic ballet. I had not danced in three years. Had it been another dance I probably would have been upset. But this is something you have do one feels "the show must go on."

Janice Barringer

PARTING IS SUCH (SOMETIMES PAINFUL) SORROW

"I was in such pain I wanted to scream."

Edward Stewart and I have traveled all over the country as free-lance artists, performing various pas de deux and concert pieces. One of our favorite and most successful pieces is an abridged version of Prokofiev's *Romeo and Juliet*. It is comprised of the balcony scene, the bedroom scene, the potion scene, and the death scene.

In the opening of the bedroom scene, Eddie and I are in bed. While I sleep, his arm is underneath my head. As he awakes, he tenderly removes his arm, kisses me, and stands up. Unfortunately, during one performance, the hooks that held his sleeve together at the wrist became caught in the mesh hair piece that was securely pinned into my hair.

At first he tried to take his arm out from under my head gently. Then he began to tug -- then harder -- and even harder. I was in such pain I wanted to scream.

Meanwhile, I'm not supposed to wake up for several more counts. Not only did I have to look asleep, but I also had to maintain a look of serenity. It was agony!

Finally, out of desperation, he gave a gigantic pull -- and a huge hunk of hair ripped out of my head.

Thank heavens for adrenalin! If it had been rehearsal, I'm not sure I could have continued.

JANICE BARRINGER, a free lance dancer, trained in Orlando, Florida, New York, and Europe. She has danced for two United States Presidents, performing as principal dancer for the Maryland Ballet, and as a permanent guest artist with the Ballet Theatre of Annapolis, Maryland. Ms. Barringer has taught for all the leading dance organizations in the country, and served on the faculty of both Harkness House and the Alvin Ailey School in New York City. She has produced a number of classroom records and one video. Her first book, "A Complete Guide to Pointe Shoes and Pointe Training" was published in 1989.

Janice Barringer and Edward Stewart

Edward Stewart

DANCING IN THE RAIN

"Before my solo, it started to rain."

We were performing Mussorgsky's *Pictures at an Exhibition*, choreographed by Robinne Comissiona at the Temple University Music Festival. It was an outdoor concert and rain was expected. As a precaution, the technicians had even covered their equipment with plastic.

It started to rain halfway into the performance, before my solo. The dancers expected Robinne to stop the performance, but she pleaded with me to do my solo first; then we would end. My solo was technically difficult and I was scared of getting injured. I argued, but did as she asked.

As I danced, cautious of every step, I was hoping the audience would make a mad dash for cover -- but no, they stayed there, sitting under umbrellas.

Before long, the stage and I were both completely soaked. As I started my final ménage of jetés, I landed on my rear. I felt both embarrassed and angry at the director for making me continue, but I sprang to my feet, finished my dance, and took my bow.

I felt like a complete jerk -- but I got a standing ovation!

EDWARD STEWART has been the artistic director and choreographer of the Ballet Theatre of Annapolis, in Maryland since 1980. He studied with the Philadelphia Civic Ballet, the Igor Youskevitch School of Ballet and the American Ballet School in New York. Mr. Stewart was a soloist with the Pittsburgh Ballet Theatre, Chicago Ballet Company, Chicago Chamber Ballet and the Maryland Ballet Company. Besides, he is a senior lecturer of Dance at Towson State University.

SHEILA REILLY studied and served as an associate teacher with the Stone- Camryn School of Ballet in Chicago. Ms. Reilly directed the National Music Camp at Interlochen for the past twenty-seven summers. She has also been the choreographer and director of ballet for the past twenty-five years in the Marquette University Theatre Arts Department, Milwaukee, Wisconsin.

on the line blazed again. The audience clapped enthusiastically. Zach took up the microphone and asked: "Now, where were we, Kristine?" -- and the audience howled. We went on to have one of our best shows.

Keeping my sanity while doing *Dreamgirls* in Los Angeles in 1983 was really difficult. Being one of the token whites in the show, I didn't have much to occupy my mischievous mind.

One girl, who should probably remain nameless (but whose first name was Tyra and whose middle name was Obnoxious) had an attitude that made her a prime target for a Yeager practical joke. At the end of the show we all played in the CCMO -- the Century City Mute Orchestra. We all held musical instruments, but we only faked playing them along with the music produced by the real orchestra. We were all pretty good at it, except for my nameless friend. She didn't want to smear her lipstick, so instead of putting the mouthpiece of her French horn to her lips, she rested it against her nose.

Well, how could I resist? One night I filled her mouthpiece with toothpaste. We watched her closely during the final section, when she just plopped the mouthpiece on her nose as usual. But, disappointingly, she didn't react. She just kept playing. Had she found the toothpaste and cleaned it out?

But when she eventually lowered the mouthpiece, a long white string of slime stretched out behind it. Her eyes got as big as saucers when she saw it growing and growing from her nose. Then, to our horror, she started screaming. (This was supposed to be a mute orchestra!) Naturally, her screams caught the attention of everyone on the stage, who immediately spotted the string of white goo and began to lose control.

Those of us who were in on the trick were more discreet and we tried to be quiet. I've done a lot of sweating in my career, but the balmiest sweat I ever broke came that night, trying to keep myself from laughing out loud.

During my two years (1985-87) in the Los Angeles company of *CATS*, we applied many touch-ups to the show to keep us all from having to go to the kitty farm. One of my favorites was what we called "Theme Night." We'd predetermine a theme for that night's show and then play with it during dull moments. One of our best themes was the JC Penney's catalogue. Whenever one of us cats had an opportunity, and was sure the theme partners were watching, we would suddenly strike a pose commonly found in the Penney's catalogue. Needless to say, we looked good. The costumes were a little strange, but the poses very familiar.

Once an understudy at the beginning of the second act forgot he was supposed to go up the stairs. He tried to step through some of the stage trash instead, but his foot caught in the chickenwire underneath. It was next to impossible keeping a straight face while the poor kitty struggled to free his paw from the wire. That darn cat. What could we do with him?

One of the most moving experiences I ever had on stage came during that *CATS* run. One night, Gregory Donaldson, who was playing the Rum Tum Tugger at the time, came off stage complaining he couldn't breathe. I told him he should take it easy, and maybe check with a doctor. The next day he went to his doctor who diagnosed a severe case of pneumonia and threw him into the hospital. His condition deteriorated very quickly, and he failed to respond to any antibiotics.

When we came in for a Saturday matinee only two short weeks later, we found the theatre blanketed in a solemn quiet. Gregory was gone.

We were stunned. He was so young, with so much to live for. We cried on each other's shoulders as we tried to come to grips with our pain. Nobody was in the mood to do a show, but we had to.

When Grizabella started to sing *Memory,* the song suddenly took on a new meaning for us: *"Touch me...It's so easy to leave me. All alone with the Memory...of my days in the sun..."* Every cat on that stage bowed his head, and tears flowed freely.

In a strange way, Gregory's passing helped us to understand the show better, and give it our best for the rest of the run.

Seung-Hae Joo

A BALCONY PAS DE DEUX

"One theatre had a lovely balcony, and we decided to use it...."

When I was dancing with the Joffrey Ballet Concert Group on one of their fall tours, our repertoire included a pas de deux from *Romeo and Juliet* in which I emerge from the bedroom onto the balcony. However, since we couldn't bring the full-sized balcony with us, we used an ugly grey box.

In one theatre, a lovely balcony jutted out into the house, and we decided to use it instead of the grey box. As the spotlight focused on me in the balcony, it spread to the people sitting in another balcony nearby.

Even so, the balcony pas de deux was believable and it was a night I'll never forget.

SEUNG-HAE-JOO received her training with the National Ballet of Korea- Sung-Namhim. After studying with the Joffrey Ballet School, she joined the Joffrey Ballet Concert Group, dancing leading roles. Ms. Joo danced in musical productions in Grand Rapids, Michigan. She has performed the grand pas de deux in *The Nutcracker* with regional ballet companies. Ms. Joo has been a soloist with Les Grands Ballets Canadiens.

Photo by: John Pregulman

141

Darla Bradle

BEING A ROCKETTE

"I'm sure the audience saw what was happening but they probably thought it was part of the show."

All the shows at the Radio City Music Hall were extravagant. During the finale of one of our spring shows, *Singing in the Rain*, it actually rained onstage. The rain was created by shooting water through holes in a pipe in the backdrop.

The scene was set in a park, and there were six trees on tracks near the front of the stage. Some of us were assigned to hide behind the trees, while others pulled us along the tracks just before it started to rain. During one performance, however, the wheels got stuck on the track, and I couldn't move my tree. I was left all by myself behind it.

The rain had already begun when a couple of singers walked over to where I was standing, on the verge of getting soaked. They simply picked up the tree -- and me! --and carried us back out of the way. I'm sure the audience saw exactly what was happening, but they probably thought it was part of the show.

The famous Radio City Christmas shows featured real animals. The holiday shows usually ran for about eight weeks, and the animal trainer- caretaker kept the beasts in temporary pens backstage for the entire run.

We had a camel, a donkey, and several sheep, and their presence made the backstage area unpleasant in more ways than one. The camel was the worst. Camels are not just unattractive, they are unfriendly -- and they don't smell very good, either. Most of the other animals were led across the stage by Music Hall people, but not the camel. Because it was so big and ornery, the animal trainer had to dress up in costume and lead it across the stage himself.

Shortly after the procession started, about ten feet onto the stage, the camel never failed to stop and pee. The trainer would do his best to get the beast going again, while the pee ran down to the footlights, causing a colorful steam to rise from the lights. We Rockettes felt lucky that we didn't have to follow that act.

DARLA BRADLE grew up in Rockford, Illinois, where she studied dance with Helen Joanne Olson. She taught dance at a local community center while still in high school. Given a successful private audition with the Rockettes, she performed with them at Radio City Music Hall in New York City for three years before moving back to Illinois to become a nurse and raise her two daughters.

Photo by: Dee Scholfield

VIVIAN TOMLINSON, a native of Cape Town, South Africa, received his early ballet training at the University of Cape Town. He was a principal dancer with the Cape Town Ballet and the Wisconsin Ballet Company, and served as artistic director of the Madison (Wisconsin) Civic Ballet. Mr. Tomlinson choreographed many musicals and operas, and staged *The Nutcracker* for the Central Wisconsin School of Ballet in Wausau, and other regional companies. He is currently teaching at the University of Wisconsin-Madison Dance Department.

Vivian Tomlinson

WITH FRIENDS LIKE THESE

"...I remember seeing the room go by in a sort of slow motion...."

In 1964, I was dancing with the University of Cape Town Ballet Company in South Africa. At the opening of *Romeo and Juliet*, I was one of three servants of the Capulet household who are headed home after a bout of drinking and are suddenly confronted by men of the house of Montague. The shock of seeing the "enemy" was supposed to bring me to such a sudden stop that I fell backwards into the arms of my two companions.

Well, one day in rehearsal, my two friends were having a private conversation at that point and had completely forgotten that they were supposed to be in the scene.

As I fell backwards, I realized -- too late -- that they were not there. By that time, there was nothing I could do.

I vividly remember seeing the room go by in slow motion before I crashed to the floor.

Needless to say, I had some strong words for my friends.

Photo by: H. Badekow

KATHLEEN REILLY, who received her early training from her father, William Reilly, won three dance scholarships from the Interlochen National Music Camp. For four years, Ms. Reilly was a member of the Hamburg Ballet Company, under the artistic direction of John Neumeier, and toured with them to the Soviet Union, South America, and all the major capitals of Europe. She joined the Ballet Met in Columbus, Ohio in 1984, becoming a soloist in 1987. In the spring of 1989, she toured with the company for two weeks in Egypt.

Kathleen Reilly

SPLIT LEAP

"We girls were all lined up along the back of the stage...looking gorgeous, watching the men march in."

When I think of all the things that have happened to me in my dancing, I must say that just being in Europe with the Hamburg Ballet Company was a highlight in my life. Dancing and traveling all over Europe was an unforgettable experience, and something I will always treasure.

That's not to say it was easy. Having to deal with the people, their different customs, language, and lifestyle was hard for me. I felt like such a foreigner, an "Ausländer." At first, I felt cut off from everyday life, mainly because I couldn't speak German. But, I forced myself to learn the language, and eventually learned to adapt to the German way of life.

Despite little traumas, I did have a good time with all of my friends in the company. My favorite story to tell took place during Act III of a performance of John Neumeier's *Sleeping Beauty*. We girls were all lined up along the back of the stage, standing in poses and looking gorgeous, watching the men march in. Now the corps de ballet are always being yelled at to stay in line, and at a certain point during the men's dance, one man had to do a monumental split-leap to get back in line. But, he not only split his leap, but also his pants which were ripped wide-open!

All of the girls in the back were laughing so hard we could hardly keep our poses. It was one thing to hear this huge tear, but to watch this poor guy trying to dance with a straight face was just too much.

I still laugh when I think about it.

I miss my friends from Hamburg. Even though we all had different backgrounds and nationalities, we still had a lot in common -- including a love for dance, and sense of humor.

DOROTHY D. LISTER, born 1934, received her early training in Pensacola, Florida, then in the Swoboda School in New York. She danced with the Ballet Russe de Monte Carlo from 1954-59, advancing from corps de ballet to soloist, and working with such legendary dancers as Maria Tallchief, Alicia Alonso, and Frederic Franklin. Ms. Lister performed at Radio City Music Hall, in musical theatre, and both on and off-Broadway. She performed in Michael Bennett's Broadway production *Ballroom* and played the role of Della in Paul Rogers' and James Coco's *Here's Where I Belong*. She has been teaching at the Joffrey Ballet School in New York since 1972.

Dorothy D. Lister

WE GAVE OUR ALL

"I slipped and slid all across the stage and into the small wing space."

When I joined the Ballet Russe de Monte Carlo in 1954, Maria Tallchief was the prima ballerina, and Frederic Franklin was the premier danseur.

We covered 108 cities in six months, traveling in two buses. The principals and the older dancers rode in the first bus, and the rest rode in the second bus with the orchestra. During these extensive travels we encountered everything from snowstorms to stages assembled with folding tables tied together.

On one occasion, we encountered such a terrible snowstorm we only arrived at the theatre at 8 p.m. curtain time. The scenery had just arrived as well, and had to be loaded in the back of the stage. That meant we had to enter through the front of the auditorium, march through the already seated audience, throw on our makeup, jog in place for a warm up, and do a performance -- all after being cramped on a bus since 8 a.m.

No one complained. We just did it, and gave our all to the audience.

In one of our many performances at small colleges, the stage was actually improvised from folding tables tied together, with heavy planks laid over them to create a floor. The wings consisted of hanging curtains, giving only about two feet of wing space. We were doing *Swan Lake*. Making our entrances, the swans had to climb up six steps before entering the stage. I was the fourth swan to enter. I slipped and slid all across the stage and into the small wing space. I got up, went around to the second wing, re- entered, and joined the group in my correct fourth space. As we danced, the loose planks moved up and down with us every time we jumped. We were very noisy little swans, but we danced on.

During a performance of *Giselle.* Marge Beddow was making her debut as the Queen of the Willis. She began her bourées and the audience began to snicker. Poor Marge thought something had fallen off her costume.

Under her veil, she could not detect the real problem. One of the local wardrobe ladies was crossing backstage to return costumes to the costume room. She was supposed to cross upstage of the back curtain, but instead was crossing between the back curtain and the scrim. She was loaded down with costumes, and walked as though she carried the weight of the world on her back. No amount of yelling or

Photo by: Maurice Seymour

149

motioning from Fred Franklin could make her move any faster, and poor Marge had to endure the commotion in the audience, not knowing what was wrong, until the wardrobe lady finally got off stage.

We always played Chicago for two weeks during Christmas, a blessedly long stand. In my first year with the company, we were doing *Ballet Imperial*. We had formed a line of nine. Three girls on each side then had to run backwards to form 1/2 a line. We smaller girls were always placed at the end, which meant we had to run faster, and farther, with our smaller legs.

We had already made our entrance when Maria Tallchief exited. She tried to warn us of a slick spot on stage left, but our group did not hear the warning. I found the spot and hit the stage, catching the full weight of my ninety-five pounds on my right hand. I landed with such force that the orchestra stopped playing for thirty seconds, trying to figure out what had happened.

I got up quickly and continued dancing, but my right hand was shaking uncontrollably. I finished the ballet in excruciating pain, with tears streaming down my face, dancing the rest of the night with a broken right wrist.

DAVID RAHER, a former member of Le Grand Ballet de Monte Carlo and, later, a founder-editor of the British journal, "<u>Dance and Dancers</u>", has been a professor of drama since 1962. For several years, he has been a visiting professor in the English Department of Seoul National University, Seoul, Korea.

David Raher

LESSONS FROM THE GREAT DANILOVA

"I slipped into the auditorium to observe the great lady as teacher..."

Some years ago, as an editor of the London periodical <u>Dance and Dancers</u>, I made an appointment to meet with the Russian ballerina Alexandra Danilova. She was at that time a guest artist with the recently formed Festival Ballet. The fledgling company was then headed by Alicia Markova and Anton Dolin.

Our rendezvous was to be her dressing room at the now defunct Stoll Theatre where the company was appearing. The interview was intended to provide me with, among other bits of information, an item for our monthly feature, "Famous Dancers' Recipes."

Wishing to be on time for our appointment, I arrived at the Stoll more than half an hour early. Told by the stage door man that Mme. Danilova was onstage, conducting a company class, I slipped into the auditorium to observe the great lady as teacher.

I had already had a taste of her special gifts as a conscientious teacher years before. When she was still a prima ballerina of the Ballet Russe de Monte Carlo, and very much in command of her performing prowess, I attended an audition she had conducted to find a replacement for the American dancer, Herbert Bliss, who had accepted an engagement on Broadway. Finally my turn came. Danilova found fault with my grand jetés. Instead of merely complaining about them, she went into elaborate detail about how they could be executed more satisfactorily. It was an excellent piece of advice, which I later used to advantage.

The class on the stage of the Stoll that morning consisted mostly of the company dancers. As I stepped unnoticed into the darkened parterre box in the auditorium, Danilova was demonstrating an allegro variation.

When the first group of dancers had performed this particular set of leaps and turns, the second group took the stage. Midway through their version of it, the heavily accented, Russian-English of Mme. Danilova broke through the evenly accented beat of the music.

"Stawp! Stawp! Stawp!" shouted Danilova. "It ees nawt pawsible dahnsing zike dat!"

She strode from her position on a stool at the footlights and addressed the front line of participants. In a controlled, gentle voice, she admonished them thus: "You are all vawnderful dahnsers. Everyting you are doing cawrect. But is nawt dahnsing vot you are doing, but exercises. You mahst give vot vee calling in New

York ..." And here she hesitated briefly, groping for the adjective with which she could make her point. "You mahst give your dahnsing more expression -- more vhat we call in New York -- schmaltz!"

The English dancers dutifully noted the advice of their revered ballet mistress, then resumed their positions on the stage. But when the pianist struck the first chord of the music, they repeated the exercise much as they had done before -- giving it only as much schmaltz as their innate British reserve would permit.

PATRICIA NEARY, born in Miami, Florida in 1942, where she received her early training. In 1957, she was asked to join the National Ballet of Canada, the youngest dancer and only American. In 1960, she joined the New York City Ballet, where she performed many principal roles in such ballets as *Apollo*, *Swan Lake*, *The Scotch Symphony* and many others. She was often described as a distinguished and dynamic soloist. Besides the full repertory of George Balanchine, she performed ballets by Jerome Robbins, Antony Tudor and John Taras. While director of the Geneva Ballet 1973-78 and of the Zurich Ballet 1978-86, Ms. Neary invited these choreographers to choreograph in Europe. Furthermore, she produced their works and the works of others. After a three year directorship of La Scala Theatre, Milan, Italy, from 1986-89, she became artistic director of Ballet British Columbia in July 1989.

Photo by: Jack Mitchell

Patricia Neary

BALANCHINE, THE MAN

"He loved life and everything about it...."

To know Mr. Balanchine, the choreographer, director and teacher, and to know George Balanchine, the man, was to know two completely different people.

The man was shy and sensitive. He loved life and everything about it, a love which is reflected in his choreography. To watch him -- like a child -- smelling spices, vegetables, and flowers -- to see him prepare a dinner like it was his greatest piece of choreography -- to watch the joy he had in selecting a superb wine and sniffing the cork!

I remember when I was in Rome, teaching a ballet of his. I phoned him to talk about the dancers, and how they should be progressing. I shall never forget his comment: "Pat, but what about Rome? What have you seen?"

I answered, "Nothing."

"Forget about my ballet!" he said. "You're only in Rome once. Go out and look at the beauty of Rome. The sculptures, the fountains, the Sistine Chapel -- Rome. Learn!"

How right he was.

PETER FONSECA, born in Washington, D.C., began his ballet training with his mother, Hortensia Fonseca. He also studied with Mary Day at the Washington Academy of Ballet and the American Ballet Theatre School. Mr. Fonseca joined the Ballet Repertory Company in the summer of 1975 and, one year later, the American Ballet Theatre, where he became soloist in 1981. Mr. Fonseca particularly enjoyed dancing George Balanchine's *Theme and Variations* and *Flower Festival* choreographed by Jerome Robbins, among others. He passed away in 1987.

Photo by: Edward Steichen
Maria Theresa Duncan, Circa 1920
Kay Bardsley Collection at Isadora Duncan International Institute

Jeanne Bresciani

MEMORIES OF MARIA-THERESA DUNCAN

"She became our dancing octogenarian."

Maria-Theresa had been slightly hard of hearing since childhood. Amazingly, it had never affected her musicality, her lyric gift. She was always able to merge with the music in a spiritual way, feeling it even more deeply and astonishingly through vibrations.

She became our dancing octogenarian, seeming to tap a source of energy unavailable to the average human being.

When a new visitor arrived at the studio, Maria-Theresa would toss her large shawl over her tunic and set out, with swaying hips, to charm the newcomer. "Come very close to me," she would say, beckoning to the visitor with a commanding flourish and a twinkle in her eye.

"I have only 'intimate' friends," she would say, winking disarmingly as she squeezed the delighted visitor's arm, and drew him near her. "One of the blessings of my Beethovenesque affliction!"

JEANNE BRESCIANI, soloist, teacher, lecturer, reconstructionist of the repertory of Isadora Duncan, has performed extensively in Europe, Canada, and America. She is regarded today as the prime interpreter of the dance legacy of Maria-Theresa Duncan, Isadora's last dancing daughter. As artist-in- residence of the Isadora Duncan International Institute, Ms. Bresciani directs studies at universities and other settings working with age groups from toddlers to oldsters. Ms. Bresciani performs regularly with Dancers for Isadora, a group she co-founded in 1980. She was a leading dancer with Isadora Duncan Commemorative Dance Company 1977-1981.

Jeanne Bresciani

INSPIRATION

"I danced as if my life depended on it."

I once had the opportunity to perform Isadora's dances of the Greek Afterlife in a benefit concert at a hospital for the terminally ill. These powerful dances portray the pain and suffering of hell and the peace and joy of heaven, and I danced as if my life depended on it, making a desperate attempt to assuage fear and anguish.

Even before the last note of music sounded, a great number of the patients struggled up from their wheelchairs, while others sat up on the tables on which they'd been wheeled in. Those who could, stamped on the floor or pounded on the metal surfaces of the tables, cheering and screaming.

I have performed on many grander stages, before and since, but no performance has ever meant more to me. It was a redemptive experience. I, too, had been transformed, as if in a baptism of fire -- and never since have I been able to conceive of dance solely as art or entertainment.

The event reminded me of Isadora's own words: " I have dreamed of a more complete dance expression ... where... the public should arise and, by different gestures ... participate in my invocation ... someday if you understand sorrow you will understand too all I have lived through, and then you will know the real Isadora is there... work and create Beauty and Harmony ... and Inspiration for a new Life."

Photo by: Lois Greenfield

163

ROBERT IVEY, born in Manly Beach, Australia in 1936, studied ballet at the American Ballet Theatre. He studied dance at the Leningrad Kirov Ballet School and pantomime in Poland. He was a member of the Swedish State Theatre 1968-75 and the Royal Norwegian Ballet from 1964-68. Mr. Ivey's credits include principal musical roles on Broadway and in Europe: Baby John in *West Side Story*, composed by Leonard Bernstein, choreographed by Jerome Robbins and Kim in *The Music Man* by Onna White. He is artistic director of the Robert Ivey Ballet and teaches dance at the College of Charleston, South Carolina.

Robert Ivey

MOGLIEV

"The next village turned out to be a mail drop named Mogliev, and it was there I stepped out into the freezing Russian night."

In 1967, I received a stipend to study pantomime with the noted Polish mime Henry Tomaszewski. I didn't know any Polish, but I felt confident that somehow or other I would be understood. After all, I had danced in Norway for several years, and was quite fluent in Norwegian, and I also had a working knowledge of German. Besides, dance and mime are international languages in themselves. To some extent, I was right to be confident. I made many friends in Poland, and quickly learned to love the country.

After I'd been in Krakow for six weeks, the Tomaszewski troupe went on tour. I was left behind, but not before they made arrangements for me to join them later. I was to travel alone by train to Warsaw, where I would change trains for the five and a half hour train ride to Gdansk. Everything was written down for me in Polish. All I had to do was match the signs with my written directions.

Everything went as planned. I arrived in Warsaw, found my train, and climbed aboard. I took a place in a compartment with several curious Poles. After what seemed like an eternity, the train lurched forward and we were on our way. No one came to take tickets, and after awhile I fell asleep.

It was dark when I awoke. I checked the time. There was another hour of travel ahead. Two hours later, I told myself we were only a little late. Then three hours passed. Four hours. I tried to question my Polish companions, who by now were getting sleepy themselves, but they couldn't understand me.

Starting to get frantic, I left the car and found a conductor, but he spoke nothing but Polish and Russian. When I tried to speak German to him, he got furious with me. Finally a young Jewish student understood my plight, and he explained everything to the conductor. Yes, I was told, I had read the sign correctly. I was on the right train, but it was going in the wrong direction. Instead of going to Gdansk, I was heading into the heart of Russia!

The next main station was Moscow, and that was still seven hours away. It was decided that I should get off the train at the next village and get the morning train from Moscow back to Warsaw. I could not simply travel on to Moscow because the Warsaw train would leave there before this train arrived.

The next village turned out to be a mail drop called Mogliev, and it was there I stepped out into the freezing Russian night. The station was closed and dark, but the

165

snow covered trees and countryside all around were shining in the moonlight. I had started to walk in search of some kind of a hotel or inn, when I saw two dark shadows coming down the road in my direction. I was as frightened as if they were the entire Russian army, but they turned out to be only a woman and a young boy. They passed by me with obvious curiosity.

I watched as they picked up the few packages left by the train, unlocked the station, and took them inside. Good, I thought. At least I'll be able to wait inside the station until morning. I ran in and tried to explain, frightening them as badly as they had frightened me. I showed them the paper the conductor had given me, explaining about my mix up with the trains and how I had slept through the border crossing.

Suddenly smiles broke across their concerned faces --big, beautiful smiles. "English!" they exclaimed. "English!" That however, seemed to be the only word they knew in the language. "Zimmer," they said, which I understood to be the German word for "room."

"Yes," I said. "*Da.*" And off we went into the snow covered night.

They took me to their home, a one room building in which the Mama, the Papa, and two sons shared everything. They gave me soup, while I warmed my feet by the fireplace. The Papa hung two quilts across the room for my privacy, and they insisted I take their best bed. I could hear them giggling and whispering long after I had crawled into it. I had taken all my Polish money to bed with me, thinking perhaps I had fallen into the hands of gypsy thieves. Little good my precautions would have done, since I slept so soundly they had to wake me in the morning.

The family had long been awake already. My boots were shining, my pants had been cleaned, and my shirt and sweater were being warmed by the fire. And even as I awoke the father was busy brushing my overcoat.

Breakfast was a feast -- tea, bread and a soft boiled egg. They watched me with eager eyes as I devoured their precious egg. All I had eaten the day before was the soup they had given me. As I realized that this must be quite a special breakfast (eggs are rare for them in the wintertime), I felt ashamed to have slept with my money and distrusted them.

They hurried me, pointing to my watch and making the wonderfully universal choo-choo sound. I dressed quickly, and they practically carried me down the road to the station. The countryside, which had been so white and romantic at night, by day was grey and barren. Like their existence, I thought. I made up my mind to add some color to it.

Over many, many objections, I gave the father my watch. Then I gave the boys some shirts and sweaters that I could never appreciate as much as they would. The mother loved my scarf and gloves. Best of all, I gave them my entire allowance for the trip of Polish money, along with thirty American dollars which are always popular on the black market.

Their tears told me all that the words I could not understand could ever tell me. The Soviet Intourist Bureau found me and took me back to Krakow that evening. Needless to say, I never tried to make connections for myself again during the rest of my stay in Poland.

I never knew their names, but I'll never forget the four members of Travelers Aid in that White Russian region somewhere between Warsaw and Moscow.

Christine Walton

ALONG CAME A SPIDER

"I felt something strange on my hand."

I was performing in a Joffrey II production of Jean Pierre Bonnefoux's Renaissance-style ballet *Madrigal*. It was a daytime performance, held outdoors, in a wooded setting. As I came on stage to meet my partner for the finale, I felt something strange on my hand. Placing the hand on his shoulder, I suddenly saw what it was -- a spider!

At this point in the choreography, I had to stand still for thirty-two counts. While I stood there, the spider kept crawling about on my fingers, tickling me. But there was nothing I could do. And even after those long, long counts were over, I could not chase the spider away. *Madrigal* is a very elegant ballet, with beautiful velvet costumes, and there was no way to shake the creature off my fingers and still maintain the sense of dignity and decorum the atmosphere demanded.

My partner could see my discomfort. And after three minutes of watching me struggle to get the spider off me, he couldn't stop himself -- he broke out laughing right there onstage.

CHRISTINE WALTON received her dance training in Montreal, Quebec, and at the Joffrey School in New York. She was a member of the Joffrey II dancers before joining the Finis Jhung Chamber Ballet U.S.A. in 1984. She performed many principal roles, among them the pas de trois in *Swan Lake*, staged by Leslie Browne and *Pastoral Quartet*, choreographed by Jeff Satinoff. In recent years, she has been with the Basel Ballet, Switzerland.

ELVIRA VECSEY, well-versed in the Vaganova Russian technique was made prima ballerina of the Budapest Opera house at the age of fifteen, after she starred in the full ballet *Sylvia*. She performed throughout Europe, and later became a ballet master. She taught, choreographed and coached in the United States for ten years before returning to her native Hungary to retire in 1985.

Elvira Vecsey

MEMORIES OF THE BUDAPEST OPERA HOUSE

"Because all the leading roles were filled, a new one was created for me."

I became a prima ballerina at the age of fifteen. I was only a student at the time, dancing at the Budapest Kings Opera House. Ptasinszky Pepi was scheduled to dance *Sylvia* with the company, but on the very day of the performance we were informed that she would be unable to come. The two other solo dancers were offered the part of Sylvia, but they turned it down. Finally Radnay Miklos offered it to me -- the leading role!

Sylvia is a difficult part, but I knew every role in the ballet, so, with as natural a voice as I could muster, I answered, "Yes, certainly."

It was a great success. Not only the public but the director and the rest of the staff loved it, too! Because all the leading roles were filled, a new one was created for me so that I could become a prima ballerina -- a title I kept until my retirement.

In my youth, I had long blond hair and looked gorgeous! One time Pataky-Kalman appeared as the guest artist at the Opera House, singing the title role in *Faust*. As I danced toward him in the first ballet scene in the opera, he astonished me by introducing himself right there on the stage.

"I am Pataky-Kalman," he announced to me.

"And I " -- I replied without hesitation -- "am Elvira Vecsey."

The audience didn't seem to notice, but I was grateful that he didn't click his heels together, as he had once done when he was a military officer before he began his career as an opera singer.

The most unusual experience I had at the Budapest Opera House came at the high point of my career there. My partner Brada Rezso and I were performing our favorite pas de deux when a lift that we had successfully performed many times before started to go wrong.

Brada's arms began to shake. And then, suddenly, after what seemed like forever, I found myself in a most unusual pose. It was very different from anything we had ever done before. But the audience was enchanted. They started to applaud, and we had to take many bows.

Later, during rehearsals, we worked for many hours to duplicate that failed lift into that mysterious pose, but it would never be seen again.

Photo by: Stephen Speidel

KATJA BIESANZ, choreographer, teacher, performer, studied dance and acting at Interlochen Arts Academy, North Carolina School of the Arts and California Arts where she received a Bachelor of Fine Arts. She won a Drama-Logue award for her role as the Feiffer Dancer in *Hold Me*. As a guest of the Ministry of Culture in Costa Rica, she performed her solo *Anima* with the National Symphony Orchestra and her *Danza del Mar* with Costa Rican National Dance Company. Recent performances include participation in Dance Kaleidoscope at the Ford Theatre in Los Angeles, and a program for the Olympic Arts Festival's International Festival of the Masks.

Katja Biesanz

THE MARRIAGE OF HEAVEN AND EARTH

"I suddenly felt inspired and compelled against all reason to create a new work...".

In 1979, I accepted an engagement to perform for the Association of Humanistic Psychology at Loyola Marymount University, as the opening event for the conference, *The Marriage of Heaven and Earth*. Given the short notice, I planned to perform only solo works from my repertoire, and began rehearsing them. Then, while at Dance Home (which is a wonderful place where people go to let loose dancing), I suddenly felt inspired and compelled against all reason to create a new work for the occasion -- in just two weeks.

A few members of my pick-up company, the Natural Movers, were present at Dance Home, and with them and others who I saw dancing there, I cast *The Marriage of Heaven and Earth* corps in minutes.

I had just met another dancer, Anna Krammer Cherakovsky, and felt she might have the right quality for one of the central figures, *Earth*. I had not yet seen her dance, but my intuition was correct: she was perfect.

Incredibly, all these people, who are usually quite busy with jobs and rehearsing, had the next two weeks completely free.

I called the composer Kevin Braheny, and he was also unexpectedly available.

The resident company of the studio I contacted for rehearsal space was on tour, and had suspended classes for that time, so the space was free.

That night I wrote a poem that would be the text for the performance. One of the dancers told me she had a friend who was a professional announcer, and who could serve as narrator. He had a wonderful voice. In rehearsal, I made a few suggestions, which he quickly implemented to wonderful effect. In performance, his timing, resonance, and interpretation were flawless. It was only after the performance that I discovered he was not a professional actor: his announcing experience was limited to calling departures at the bus terminal. He had been absolutely terrified, but was bolstered by my confidence in him.

On the way to the performance, I remembered that in the rush I had neglected to find any little performance gifts for the cast. I had only two carnations someone had given me, and on a Sunday night, with only three dollars in my pocket, it seemed unlikely that I could come up with anything. But there in the twilight, on the freeway off-ramp, a boy lingered late, hoping to sell his last bunch of flowers. The price was exactly three dollars.

The bouquet consisted of five red and four white roses, one for each dancer wearing that color. I gave the carnations to the composer and the narrator.

The venue was a gymnasium. Logistics, time, and finances precluded elaborate lighting. Turning that liability into an asset, we had decided to involve the audience by having them define the performance space by standing in an enormous circle, holding candles for the light. When I arrived, I found not only that circle, but all the pathways and floor patterns of the dance, painted on the floor in red and white, the school colors.

The audience passed the flame from candle to candle, creating a soft glow. The walls disappeared, and the space was transformed. Just as we stepped in place to begin the dance, the clouds moved, and bright moonlight streamed down upon us through the gymnasium's skylight, making the whole dance area a luminous circle.

The performance was the smoothest I had ever experienced, and passed like an inspired trance.

At the last moment of the dance, as the audience blew out the candles, the clouds covered the moon, and it did not come out again that night.

Somehow I feel I was not making this dance alone.

Photo by: Kenn Duncan

DAVID ANDERSON danced with the San Francisco Ballet, the American Ballet Theatre, and in the original Broadway cast of *Applause*. Mr. Anderson taught at the Joffrey Ballet School in New York. As a choreographer, his work has been commissioned by the Joffrey II Dancers, the Hubbard Street Dance Company, and Iwanson Dance of Munich, Germany. He was a recipient of a 1979 National Endowment of the Arts Choreography Fellowship.

David Anderson

SHOWING OFF

"Preparing for the prom, the Demolays had soaped the floor to make it slick."

My partner Judy and I were dancing before a prom in my hometown of San Antonio, Texas, about 1958. I hadn't been dancing for very long at that point in my career, but I thought that I was sensitive to what a performing situation was. We chose "Harlem Nocturne" for our music. It sounded sexy, and I loved it.

I wore black pants, a black turtleneck, and black ballet slippers. Judy wore black tights and slippers, with a dark blue leotard and skirt with a slit up the side. With her bright red hair, she looked great. We choreographed the dance to be as sexy as the music, and we both felt that the steamy atmosphere we planned to create really fit us.

We were prepared to show off! We took our places for the opening, with Judy behind me and both of us in second position. Now, in second position your feet are supposed to be apart. Except that in this case our feet kept getting wider and wider apart, gradually sliding across the floor!

Preparing for the prom, the Demolays had soaped the floor to make it slick. That way, your partner was forced to cling to you, whether he or she wanted to or not.

Only what worked to make things sexier for slow-dancing couples at a prom had the opposite effect for the more elaborate sexiness we had in mind. Our "Harlem Nocturne" proceeded all too cautiously, to say the least.

At the climax of the dance, Judy came running to me. I lifted her at the waist and hoisted her up into a position in which her back rested against my shoulder, with her head behind me and her feet extended in front. I hunched over to get as much resistance as the slippery floor would give. But my change in position caused her to slide right down my back. Luckily, I caught her by the feet and shins before she slithered all the way down to the floor. But that left Judy hanging there like a sack of potatoes.

To save face, I spun around (as fast as I could in my hunched position) with Judy flapping behind me. I finished with a quick forward motion that allowed Judy to contract her body up, and then scramble to her feet -- all of which provided a surprisingly successful finish to an embarrassing disaster.

We acknowledged our applause. Then we went off to cry for about an hour.

ELAINE SUMMERS, born in Australia, was raised in Boston, Massachusetts. She received her Bachelor of Science degree from the Massachusetts College of Arts. Ms. Summers studied dance at the Juilliard School and at the Martha Graham Studio before becoming a member of the Janet Collins Dance Company. Later, she became part of the Judson Dance Theatre. In 1962, Ms. Summers began combining dance with film and slides, quickly gaining a reputation for her innovative film making. Ms. Summers has received many grants, including one in 1989 to study 8 mm films on dance in Italy.

Elaine Summers

MOVABLE STATUES

"Once I was arranged in a position, I was not to move."

One of the strangest things that ever happened to me as a dancer occurred during a performance of *The Queens's Dog*, a piece choreographed by Carolee Schneemann and performed at the Judson Church in the early 1960's.

Carolee's idea was the male projecting onto the woman. A male dancer would manipulate the women in various positions, projecting himself onto them, and defining their physicality in space. The women were being created, as if from clay or mud.

My part required that I remain very still, yet movable. Once I was arranged in a position, I was not to move.

During one performance, a member of the audience was intent on disturbing my immobility. Whoever it was threw a glass of water in my face, and then, later in the dance, a tomato.

I, of course, did not move a muscle. If I recall correctly, I did not even blink.

Kathryn Stephenson

A WAD OF LACE

"I looked back in horror! The lace on my skirt had become attached to a girl going in the opposite direction."

In the early 1970s, I was dancing in a Disney on Parade show called *The Three Caballeros* on the west coast. I was one of sixteen girls in a big cancan number. We each wore an elaborate skirt, with layers and layers of lace, made up of a single piece of the material about 21 inches wide.

Some 30 seconds into the piece, we would form a long line, and then, after some fast foot work and a lot of swishing of skirts, each of us would take off in a different direction. We had to move quickly, taking long running steps, until we were approximately 36 feet apart. But in one performance I'd only made it about 20 feet when I was pulled to a stop. I was literally "hung up" there. I couldn't move another step.

I looked back in horror!

The lace on my skirt had gotten attached to a girl going in the opposite direction, and now it was stretched out between us, tying us together! I gave it a tug, thinking that might release it. But it wasn't going to be that simple. Even several more emphatic yanks failed to set it free.

The next formation was a block. Luckily, the two of us were side-by- side. She managed to pull my new "train" off the hook on the back of her costume where it had gotten caught. That solved her problem. But I was left to gather up the yards and yards of lace that lay tangled at my feet.

I had to continue dancing carrying this big wad of lace. By then, the whole corps was laughing so hysterically that we were getting weak in the knees. When it came time for the diagonal kick line, I needed both arms to do shoulder-to-shoulder. I had to let go of my hoard of material to keep it from getting wrapped around not just me but, both of my neighbors as well. Even so, the final jump split took place in a sea of black and white lace!

Photo by: Maurice Seymour

BILLIE MAHONEY, a revered tap dancer, teacher, and choreographer, was a featured artist on the Ed Sullivan Show, the Tonight Show, and other popular television programs of the 1950s. Her varied career includes several musical comedy appearances: *Pal Joey* with Bob Fosse (1961), *Hit the Deck* with Gene Nelson (1960) and *Song of Norway* with Robert Rounsville (1958-1959). She has also appeared with comedian Bob Hope and vibraphonist musician Lionel Hampton with whom she toured Korea and Japan for the U.S.O. in 1953. Ms. Mahoney was the head of the Department of Labanotation in the Dance Division of the Juilliard School for fifteen years beginning in 1958. She was appointed the head of the dance division of the University of Northern Illinois in 1989.

Billie Mahoney

TELL ME ABOUT IT!

"A few days before I was to leave, all the newspapers and magazines were full of photographs of Viscountess de Ribes ... with a young Soviet dancer who had defected from the Kirov Ballet."

Whenever students get depressed because of missed jobs, auditions, or other unrealized opportunities, I say, "Tell me about it!"

In the spring of 1961, Raymundo de Larrain, the nephew of Marquis de Cuevas, had just choreographed a spectacular *Sleeping Beauty* for the Grand Ballet du Marquis de Cuevas in Paris. He had been invited to stage his new ballet, *Entre Chat*, for the Embassy Ball, a charity affair annually held at the Waldorf Astoria in New York.

At that time, I was appearing as the drum majorette, leading the band and a host of elephants, with the Ringling Brothers Circus at Madison Square Garden. The Marquis de Larrain saw my performance and, after a private audition, invited me to be the Turquoise Cat in his new ballet.

It was an exciting three weeks of rehearsals, doing challenging tricks and putting my ballet training to use. Costumes were designed by de Larrain himself, and my shoes were flown in from Paris. Stars from the Paris Opera Ballet and the de Cuevas Ballet were brought to New York for the two twenty- minute performances at the Waldorf Astoria.

After the Embassy Ball performances were over, de Larrain observed some of the jazz classes I was teaching. He decided to turn the twenty-minute *Entre Chat* into a full length jazz ballet.

He asked me to be co-choreographer, as well as to perform as guest artist in the ballet. I was to give the de Cuevas dancers daily jazz dance lessons to prepare them for new style of dance. A three-month tour was booked, opening in Beauville and ending on the French Riviera. Having majored in French in college, and having dreamed of someday touring France as a performer, this opportunity was the realization of all my dreams.

I completed a three week engagement at the City Center Theatre with Bob Fosse in *Pal Joey*, had a new wardrobe made, and was ready for my Parisian debut as both choreographer and dancer. De Larrain had called a couple times from Paris to confirm aspects of the agreement. Everything was set. I had only to wait for my ticket to France.

A few days before I was to leave, all the newspapers and magazines were full of photographs of Viscountess de Ribes walking arm in arm with a Soviet dancer named Rudolph Nureyev, who had defected from the Kirov Ballet. The young sensation was to appear with the de Cuevas Ballet.

Shortly after, a polite letter arrived stating that, due to "certain obligations contracted by the company", the jazz ballet was being "postponed." I would be notified when a new date was set.

De Cuevas never did the jazz ballet. And, no doubt much to his chagrin, the company survived less than a year after Nureyev began dancing with them.

Betty Shuford Zeps

HURRICANE RUDOLPH

"We, of course, had heard about his temper and his unremitting habits, and we were ready for the worst."

Being with the Wisconsin Ballet Company in the spring of 1974 was akin to being in the eye of a passing hurricane. Hurricane Rudolph to be precise. And I, as costumer and costume designer for the Ballet was as much affected as was Tibor Zana, the company's artistic director.

All winter long we had been busy preparing for the appearance of Rudolph Nureyev with the Wisconsin Ballet. Many other famous names in ballet -- including Margot Fonteyn, Edward Villella, Natalia Makarova, Ivan Nagy, Gelsey Kirkland, and Peter Martins, among others -- had appeared with the company, but Rudolph would be the first to actually dance a ballet with our soloists, and using our dancers as the corps. It was to be one of his first appearances with a "regional ballet." We, of course, had heard about his uncertain temper and his unremitting habits, and we were ready for the worst.

A squall blew up even before he arrived. The ballet was to be *Les Sylphides*, which required us to order many new long, white tutus from our seamstresses. But to our horror, the tutus came back in a variety of wrong lengths. Worse, most of them had been put together backwards! My assistant Betty Reddan weathered the squall, and somehow made sure we had the tutus ready before Rudolph arrived. But what was not ready was the costume I was supposed to be making for Rudolph.

I had been waiting for his measurements. I had been assured that the Ballet's Chairman of the Board had taken them at one of the meetings between them. But no measurements ever arrived. So, when Rudolph himself appeared, there was no costume waiting for him.

I took his measurements myself, telling him in my best no-nonsense, no-doubt-about-it way that his new costume would be ready two days before we opened at the Performing Arts Center in Milwaukee. Of course, he didn't believe me. He called Lynn Seymour who was still in London preparing to leave for Madison, and asked her to bring him the black jacket with white, pure silk sleeves he had used dancing *Les Sylphides* with the Royal Ballet.

Lynn soon arrived with the costume. What joy when we finally entered the Performing Arts Center for dress rehearsal at about 11 o'clock on the morning of the first performance. Maybe (we told ourselves, without quite believing it) Hurricane Rudolph would pass with very little damage after all. But we were deluding ourselves.

At 3 o'clock the long awaited storm finally hit. It struck in the form of a new backdrop that Nureyev had brushed up against countless times during the rehearsal. It had been painted with aniline, a blue dye that colors almost anything that touches it -- permanently. Those beautiful white silk sleeves were now a bright, shining blue!

His dresser was frantic, and the Nureyev temper was churning very close to the surface.

Why hadn't the painter sprayed the backdrop with a fixer? We had no time to think about that. There was nothing to do but make a new set of sleeves and put them into the costume. But it was obvious that if we used silk again we would be making new sleeves before every performance. I talked with Rudolph -- Could we use a synthetic? Only in an emergency. Well, I decided, this was an emergency. How much of an emergency, I was still to learn.

By this time, it was already close to 4:30 and we had an 8 o'clock curtain. Even more urgently, downtown Milwaukee stores close at 5:30 on Saturday afternoon. I ran the three blocks to the nearest fabric store, looking for a white silk-like polyester, a reasonable facsimile of the sleeves then in the costume. Nothing. They were sold out. On up the street. Same result. Finally, many blocks from the theatre, I found a store that had what we needed. There was even a display of the fabric right there in its window - - but the store was closing its doors. I pleaded with the storekeeper who kindly let me in and sold me the fabric. I rushed back to the theatre feeling triumphant.

But it was now 6:30. We had a scant hour and a half left. I have never cut and sewn so fast, before or since. A Nureyev performance only comes along once for most of us, however, and with Betty Reddan on one side of the jacket and me on the other we removed and dismantled the sleeves so that we could construct a pattern.

Nureyev's dresser appeared in the doorway. We shooed him away, telling him that the costume would be ready by the time the warm-up was finished. After all, we still had twenty minutes to go before he was to go on stage.

I cut one sleeve and started sewing. Betty cut the other and handed it to me. She sewed on buttons while I finished the second sleeve. With Betty again on one side of the jacket and myself on the other, we frantically stitched the sleeves back on.

The audience was seated, the orchestra was playing the introduction and Nureyev was standing impatiently in the wings, as I calmly handed the beautifully resleeved jacket to his dresser, who quickly fitted it on him.

We had done our best to make this *Les Sylphides* beautiful. The rest was up to Nureyev, as Hurricane Rudolph swept onto the stage.

BETTY SHUFORD ZEPS held an assistantship in costuming while studying for her M.A. in Theatre Theory at Indiana University, before going on to further extensive graduate training at the University of Wisconsin in Madison. Ms. Zeps has been costumer for the Madison Theater Guild and the Wisconsin Ballet Company, and gave a major costume seminar at the Midwest Ballet Festival in Detroit, Michigan. She is currently costume consultant to both CTM Productions and the Central Wisconsin Ballet School in Wausau.

TIME

JOFFREY BALLET'S "ASTARTE"

HERBERT MIGDOLL

TRINETTE SINGLETON was born in Beverly, Massachusetts, where she studied dance until graduation from high school. In 1965, she joined the Joffrey Ballet and soon after was promoted to principal dancer. She retired in 1980. In 1967 she created the title role in *Astarte*, the multi-media ballet (the first to make the cover of <u>Time</u> magazine), choreographed by Robert Joffrey. In 1982, she became the assistant ballet mistress for the Joffrey Ballet and in 1984 joined the teaching staff of the Joffrey School, Edith D'Addario, executive director. She has choreographed two works, *Awakening* and *Three by Six*, music by Bill Washer (her husband).

Photo by: Herbert Migdoll

Dean Badolato

A NIGHT TO REMEMBER

"It was as if Busby Berkeley had come alive for an evening."

On September 29, 1983, *A Chorus Line* broke the record and became the longest running Broadway show in history. Michael Bennett, who not only thought up the idea for the now legendary show but also directed and choreographed it, celebrated the event by adding about 350 *Chorus Line* veterans to the cast for the record-breaking performance.

I was working in *On Your Toes* at the time, and so I was fortunate enough to participate in the extravaganza. What's more, my parents were in town that weekend, so we all got to experience it together.

With so many dancers taking part in the show that night, Michael had to rent the Booth Theatre, which connects to the Shubert where *A Chorus Line* was playing, as a dressing room for the all the extra dancers. In order for entrances and timing to be right for those of us dressing next door in the Booth, Mr. Bennett had a giant 20-foot by 20-foot video screen hung in there, to carry the show live from the theatre next door.

I shared the balcony of this "dressing room" with people from eight or nine different companies of *A Chorus Line*, including the Japanese, Australian, and British national tours. It was an incredible sight -- as if Busby Berkeley had come alive for an evening.

Michael had Shubert Alley carpeted in beige -- the show's dominant color -- for the party afterwards. A silk tent provided a new canopy for the famous alleyway. Pictures of all 350 Chorus Line-ers were hung along the Alley's wall. Each of our names was individually flashed in neon lights across the Shubert marquee -- and this lasted the entire day and evening!

I still have my silver top hat to commemorate the event. It was truly a great evening for the theatre. I have never seen or felt any theatrical celebration to compare to it, not ever, and I can't imagine there will be another evening like it for a long, long time.

Unlike most of the previous longest-running shows, which closed soon after breaking the record, *A Chorus Line* is still kicking -- still playing to full houses six years after setting the new record.

CHERYL YEAGER, born in Washington, D.C., was trained at the School of the Maryland Ballet. In 1976, she joined the American Ballet Theatre as a member of the corps de ballet, a soloist in 1981, and a principal dancer in 1987. Among the many ballets she danced are: *Donizetti Variations*, *Don Quixote*, (Kitri's Wedding), *Duet*, and in *Etudes*. Leading roles were created for Ms. Yeager by Clark Tippet in his *Bruch Violin Concerto No. 1* and by Lynne Taylor-Corbett in her *Great Galloping Gottschalk*.

Cheryl Yeager

EMBARRASSMENTS

"I ran onstage, only to find that half the corps was still there."

I have been embarrassed twice while dancing in Marius Petipa's *Don Quixote*. My first solo with American Ballet Theatre was as the little Cupid in *Don Quixote*. It should have been a doubly-wonderful occasion for me -- since it took place in my hometown, Washington, D.C. Unfortunately, it was doubly embarrassing.

I had less than a week to prepare, because I was replacing a girl who had been injured. That first night, the girl stayed with me in the wings to help with my entrances. I was nervous, but she was very calm and supportive.

I got through everything, except my final variations, without making any mistakes. As I waited eagerly for my last entrance, I was exhausted, but very pleased with what I had done. Then I thought I heard the girl say, "Yes, it is time."

I ran onstage, only to find that half the corps was still there. I tried to stop short, but slipped and fell. I sat there in shock. All my friends and relatives were there to watch my debut as a soloist, and there I was, at center stage -- on my buns. Mortified, but not knowing what else to do, I crawled off the stage.

The second embarrassment came later in my career, by which time I was able to handle it better. By then I was dancing Kitri. It is a demanding role, and I was scheduled to dance on Sunday with Martine van Hamel dancing on Saturday. But Martine got injured and I was thrust into doing both performances.

Everything went well on Saturday night. On Sunday, however, I was tired and worried about dancing again so soon. Despite my worries, things went so smoothly on Sunday that I began to feel, while dancing, that it was one of my better performances. Everything was working, and I felt really relaxed. In the third act, I did one of the best pas de deux that I had ever done. Then I went onstage for my variation, carrying a fan that was an important prop in that part of the dance.

I stopped in fifth position, prepared to go into the échappé. With a great sense of confidence and authority, I raised my fan -- and promptly dropped it.

It lay there on the floor in front of me. Of course, I could not simply grab it. That would throw off the timing of the dance. But at the same time, there was no way I could finish the variation without it.

Luckily, the conductor was watching me, and he stopped the orchestra.

I looked at him.

I looked at my fan.

Staying in fifth position, I bent forward and picked up the fan with my right hand. I looked straight at the audience as I flipped open the fan. The conductor started the orchestra, and I went on with the variation.

I would never have believed such a thing could happen to me. But, thanks to experience -- and an observant conductor -- everything worked out.

ANNE MARIE HOLMES, Canadian born, has performed and taught ballet in over thirty countries on five continents. She and her ex-husband, David Holmes, were the first North Americans invited to dance with the Kirov Ballet in Leningrad. Several major dance films were created about them, including the award winning documentary *Tour en l'Air* and Norman McLaren's special effects short, *Ballet Adagio*. Many contemporary works have been created for her by choreographers such as Rudi Van Dantzig, Jorge Lefebre, Brian MacDonald, Agnes de Mille and others. She set the entire *Don Quixote* and *Giselle* for the Boston Ballet before rising to assistant to the director, Bruce Marks, in 1989. Ms. Holmes was ballet mistress with the Boston Ballet from 1985 to 1989. In the spring of 1988, she was presented with a medal of honor in Leningrad. The award was in recognition of her long association with the school and the Kirov Ballet.

Anne-Marie Holmes

A BITE OF THE APPLE

"When I bit into the apple, my tooth got stuck."

The strangest thing that ever happened to me was while I was dancing *Firebird* with the London Festival of Ballet in 1967.

I was in the process of having a tooth capped. At one point in the ballet, I was to bite into an apple and throw it offstage. Well, when I bit into the apple, the capped tooth got stuck.

I had two choices. I could dance the rest of the ballet with the apple hanging from my mouth, or pull the tooth out with the apple and throw them both offstage. That, of course, is what I did.

But then, of course, I had to keep my mouth closed for the entire performance.

INDIGNITIES

"I could tell that Anton was incensed ... ."

Anton Dolin and I went to a party given for the dancers of Les Grands Ballets Canadiens one night after a performance. I was a guest artist with the company at the time, and Anton had choreographed the ballet that night. Surprisingly, considering the occasion, most of the hosts said nothing about either my performance or Anton's choreography.

I could tell that Anton was incensed by this strangely rude behavior. "Anne-Marie, get your coat," he said. "We are leaving."

That was fine with me. My coat had been put upstairs and I went up to get it. On the way down, I slipped at the top of the stairs and bumped on my bottom all the way down to the very last step.

Everyone stared at me.

Anton rushed over, now even more upset because no one else had made a move to help me. He took me by the arm and helped me up. Filled with indignation and some embarrassment, we strode to the door, flung it open and rushed out -- only to find ourselves in a large closet!

CAUGHT!

"The audience must have been able to hear a moaning noise coming from behind the cross."

Natasha Makarova and I alternated the title role of *Giselle* with the National Ballet of Holland in Amsterdam.

You probably know that Giselle goes mad and dies. In the second act her spirit emerges from the grave. However, in this performance, the cross that covers the grave of Giselle was different from the one that Natasha and I were used to. As opposed to opening the side, the cover on the grave opened in the middle.

During dress rehearsal, as the spirit of Giselle emerged from the grave, Natasha's skirt got caught in the opening as the two parts of the cross closed upon it. She had to tug unbecomingly at it to get it free. I made a mental note to be careful not to get my own skirt caught.

I leaned forward to make sure that my skirt was clearing the opening. It was. But as I looked down the cover to the grave closed, not on my skirt but on my nose!

The audience must have heard a strange moaning noise from behind the cross. At least the stagehands did, for they realized what had happened and lifted the cross slightly: just enough to free the otherworldly Giselle from an embarrassingly earthly problem.

ST. CARLOS

"The stagehand was on his knees, looking up at me... ."

I was dancing *Romeo and Juliet*, a ballet choreographed by Rudi van Dantzig, with the National Ballet of Holland. We were performing at the St. Carlos Opera House in Portugal, which has one of the most heavily raked stages in all of Europe. Because of the steep angle, stagehands had to hold on to the set during the performance or it would have slid straight down into the orchestra pit.

At one point, I was supposed to run to a door, throw it open and look out in search of Romeo. But in one performance the door stuck. I stepped back a little and pulled harder, but no luck. It simply would not open.

In the next performance, I was determined to make sure the door would open. I ran to it and pulled with all my force -- I pulled so hard that the stagehand who'd been holding the door in place was yanked right out onto the stage. The whole set shook back and forth. It would probably have toppled over, but luckily someone else grabbed it and held it up.

The stagehand was on his knees, looking up at me in horror like a peeping Tom caught staring into Juliet's window.

We froze there for an endless second before he recovered sufficiently to crawl offstage on his knees.

PATRICIA WILDE began her career at the age of fourteen with the Marquis de Cuevas Ballet
International. The following year, she joined the Ballet Russe de Monte Carlo where she performed
solo roles. Ms. Wilde was a principal dancer with the New York City Ballet for fifteen years, dancing
every major female role in the company's repertoire, many of which were created for her by Mr.
Balanchine. She was later associated with the American Ballet Theatre for twelve years, where she
served as ballet mistress and coach before being appointed to the directorship of the company's school.
She is currently artistic director of the Pittsburgh Ballet Theatre.

Patricia Wilde

A RELAXING EVENING

"Symphony Concertante had three long movements, and we only had time to practice the first."

I joined the New York City Ballet for its first tour to Covent Garden in 1950. I was told to understudy everything.

I danced the fourth movement in the opening performance of *Symphony in C.* That night, Maria Tallchief injured her foot in the first movement, which meant that the following evening I had to dance the first movement as well as the fourth. That left me no time to relax, and I wondered if the entire season was going to continue this way.

Eventually, however, I was scheduled to have a free evening. Madame Karsavina was giving a tea in honor of the company at the Royal Society Circle. I arrived at four o'clock, prepared to enjoy my first relaxing evening since getting to London.

About an hour later somebody came up to me and asked if "Mr. B." had seen me. "Mr. B.," of course, was George Balanchine.

"No," I said.

"Well, he's looking for you."

Like a fool, I went to find him.

"You know Tanny had an infected corn removed from her foot today," he told me. "So I thought you should do *Symphony Concertante* for her tonight."

"But, I've never had a rehearsal!" I protested. "Mr. Balanchine, you don't mean it."

"Go to the theatre," he insisted, in his confident voice. "I will have Lew Christiansen, Maria Tallchief, and Todd Bolender come, and you can learn it before the performance."

Oh, dear, I thought. It's already after five, and the performance begins at seven! I rushed for a taxi.

Symphony Concertante had three long movements, and we only had time to practice the first before the performance. Luckily, I was dancing the second voice, with Maria dancing the first. That meant that I could watch her dance her part, and then do the same thing she had done, only in reverse. But when we got to the Adagio, it was a different story. We hadn't even had a chance to talk about it before the performance, much less to rehearse it.

199

Maria and Todd literally talked me through the entire piece. "Now do pique arabesque and hold it," Maria would say. And Todd would say, "Developé and rond-de jambe to attitude." I know that's how it happened, but I don't really remember a thing about the whole performance.

Still -- and despite the fact that I was upset with myself for being foolish enough to search out Mr. Balanchine at the party -- it never entered my mind to say, "I can't do it."

WAXED FLOORS

"The trouble came right away."

In 1947, a Ballet Russe de Monte Carlo tour took us to a Catholic university in the midwest. We had no portable floor in those days, and the people at the university had waxed the stage to make it nice for us.

The trouble came right away. Bobby Lindgren danced the Gigue at the very beginning of George Balanchine's *Mozartiana*, and at his exit, he was to run off stage, while all the girls entered with a big pas de chat. They were to land in a typical Balanchine position, hips forward and upper body leaning back.

Bobby slipped making his exit. Meanwhile, seven out of eight of the girls sailed out from the wings to land fanny down on the shiny waxed floor -- just as Bobby came sliding in among them.

DANILOVA ON HORSEBACK RIDING

*"One day while on tour in Arizona, a few of us went horeseback riding.
Danilova was furious."*

When I joined Ballet Russe de Monte Carlo in 1945, Mr. Balanchine worked a great deal with the company. Marie Jeanne, Nicolas Magallanes and I had the lead roles in the first performance of his *Concerto Barocco*.

One day while on tour in Arizona, a few of us, including Maria Tallchief, went horseback riding. Alexandra Danilova was furious with us when she found out. "How can you dance when you have been riding?" she demanded.

As was often the case on tour in those days, it happened that we had a slippery stage that night. There was a point in *Serenade* when Maria Tallchief was to jump into Nick's arms over two girls who were lying on the stage. As she started her jump, she stepped on one of the girl's skirts, and, suddenly, instead of soaring up, she was sliding down. Nick just managed to scoop her up and save her from disaster.

Danilova, of course, blamed the slip on horseback riding. "Do you see what happens when you go riding?" she scolded. "You fall and ruin the performance."

The next ballet was *Danse Concertes*, in which Danilova and Frederic Franklin performed together, and Maria, Nick and I did the pas de trois. When Danilova came out, she skidded across the waxed and slippery floor.

From the wings I heard Nick gasp, "Oh no!" The rest of us held our breath as Danilova recovered and went on.

One thing was for certain -- no one dared to ask Danilova if she had gone horseback riding.

PATTI COLOMBO was born in San Francisco, California, where she began her career in the theatre. After two and a half years at the New York School of Performing Arts, she worked in regional theatres throughout the country, performing such roles as Adelaide in *Guys 'n Dolls*, Charity in *Sweet Charity* and Lois/Bianca in the revival of *Kiss Me Kate* at the Old Globe Theatre in San Diego. She has also performed the role of Val in the international tour of *A Chorus Line*. Her choreographic credits include the opening of *Videopolis* at Disneyland, *Brigadoon*, *Meet Me in St. Louis* and *Grease*. She has won Drama-Logue awards for *Desert Song*, *West Side Story* and the San Francisco hit show, *Dance Between the Lines*. Most recently Ms. Colombo choreographed the new night club *Mannequins* for Disney.

Patti Colombo

THANK YOU

"Now it was time for me to put my money where my mouth was."

I came back from New York City like a dog with her tail between her legs. That "prestigious" acting school and I just didn't hit it off. After breaking into the theatre, being the main focus of my life, I had failed survival in the "Big Apple". It hadn't been at all like the New York portrayed in *That Girl*, or in all those movies. It was tough there, and I was a "wimp".

I was in my early twenties. I was a mess. So-o, back to beautiful safe Marin County, California, my boyfriend, friends, and family. Now, I'll be happy!

I wandered through a couple years of my life teaching in a girls' school, trying to fit in, and kind of dancing. It was all well and good until *A Chorus Line* (the original cast) took San Francisco by storm. It was the musical of musicals and it was about dancers -- about me. I saw that show and cried, screamed and applauded. It touched my innermost being. I desperately wanted to be in that show. I knew I could be "Val", and I told everyone so.

Then one day the San Francisco Chronicle carried a full page ad about an open audition for *A Chorus Line*.

The "jig" was up. I had been yapping to everyone how much I wanted to be in that show. Now it was time for me to put my money where my mouth was.

But, I didn't want to go. I hadn't been dancing a lot. I was chunky and out of shape and (get this) I couldn't find a leotard (Oh, come on! I had tons of them). My mom said, "If you don't go, I'll never believe that you really want to do this...."

I went.

There were hundreds of girls in the basement of the Curran Theatre. We went in groups of ten.

"Double pirouettes everyone." The first girl was about fifty pounds over-weight (and obviously not a dancer) she couldn't do the turn. Michael Bennett asked her why she was there. She said she was a "singer". He said this is a dancers' show. Thank you very much.

I made it through the ballet combination and ballet was not my thing. I was a jazz dancer! On to the jazz. No sweat, that is until I psyched myself out of doing a triple turn (I could always do them in class.) I freaked! I was in the back, sweating profusely, shaking, thinking that I was, after all, too fat, not right -- just forget it. (All the things that can go through your mind in an audition).

Then I was stumbling through this turn and Michael Bennett, like a God parting the waves, came toward me. He came right up to me and said, "Patti," (God, he knew my name), "you can do this -- now do it." I did it. And I did it perfectly. He said, "Thank you" and walked away.

I got the role of Val. It changed my life.

No, thank <u>you</u>, Michael Bennett.

LANCE WESTERGARD made his professional debut at the Metropolitan Opera House in a role especially created for him in Antony Tudor's *In His Concerning Oracles*. A graduate of the Juilliard School, he has performed and taught in the United States and all over the world. He has choreographed for several companies including the Joffrey II Dancers (where he was ballet master) and the Contemporary Dance Company of Hong Kong. He is noted for his solo concert *Moves*, a survey of modern dance in the 20th century.

Lance Westergard

SUMMER STOCK WITH GOLDIE

"Goldie was laughing, the audience was laughing, and I was stomping on a rubber chicken... ."

Back in 1965, I was doing *Kiss Me, Kate,* on the Guder-Ford-Gross summer stock circuit on the east coast. One night we were performing in a tent in Owings Mills, Maryland. My partner in several dance sequences was a young actress named Goldie Hawn. One of our dances was a tarantella that came shortly after a scene in which a rubber chicken was supposed to fall from the light grid above the stage. On this particular night, the chicken got caught on a light and didn't make it to the stage. That was one lost joke -- or so we thought.

I had Goldie on my shoulder in the middle of our tarantella when, behold!, the chicken finally came down from the rafters. It hit Goldie on the head and fell to the floor right under my feet. In a few seconds Goldie was laughing, the audience was laughing, and I was stomping on a rubber chicken. To top everything off, I suddenly realized that the shoulder of my red velvet jacket was turning dark red -- and wet. Goldie was totally out of control!

The poor lady couldn't help it. And the scene wasn't over yet! At the end of the dance we had to sit on the edge of the stage while the leading lady, Patrice Munsel, sang a ballad, *"I'm Afraid that Women are so Simple."*

It had to be 98 degrees in the tent. What's more, we were performing in a theater-in-the-round. There were no wings to run into, no upstage or downstage -- in short, no place to go, and nothing to do but grin and bear it. Indeed we did. But, although we were supposed to look amorously at each other, I remember Goldie and I (young professionals that we were) biting our tongues while tears rolled down our cheeks.

Photo by: Jack Mitchell

WALTER CAMRYN, born in Helena, Montana, 1903, studied with Adolph Bolm, Alexandra Maximova, Vecheslav Swoboda, among others, was a première danseur and choreographer with the Chicago Civic Opera Company and a soloist with the Page-Stone Ballet. He also taught at the Chicago-based Stone-Camryn School, that produced many professional dancers. Mr. Camryn has choreographed some twenty ballets, including *Roundelay* (Ravel), *Thunder in the Hills* (Foster, 1939), *Symphony in C* (Haydn, 1944), *Hansel and Gretel* (Humperdinck, 1934), and *In My Landscape* (Aborn, 1960).

Walter Camryn

PAVLOVA

"No name in the dance world meant as much."

We had just finished our 9 a.m. class, when our ballet master, Laurent Novikoff, received the tragic news that Anna Pavlova had died of double pneumonia in The Hague, Holland. We all gathered around Mr. Novikoff, who had been her partner for many years, as he reminisced about her and her importance in the dance world. Four other members of our company at that time had also danced in Pavlova's company, so we all felt a deep sense of shock, as if we had lost a personal friend. And, in a sense, we had. All of us had seen her dance at least once in our student years. No name in the dance world meant as much.

I first saw her dance in Boise, Idaho, and if my memory serves me correctly she danced her "California Poppy," her "Gavotte," and a demi- character number in an exquisite Russian costume. The ballet that evening was *Amarilla*.

The impression of her that stays most persistently in my mind, however, is of a movie I once saw at Jacob's Pillow of her dancing her "Dragonfly." Even in this old movie one got a wonderful feeling toward this unearthly creature of dance.

So much of my early dance life was spent close to people who had been associated with Pavlova. My first teacher Adolph Bolm had been her first partner out of Russia in 1907, and he had told us many stories of their tour to Stockholm, Copenhagen, Prague and Berlin. Later, I studied with Muriel Stuart, who had been reared by Pavlova and was one of her important soloists.

We owe more to Pavlova than to any other artist for the popularity of ballet in the world today. She pioneered through practically every civilized country in the world, places where people were seeing this art for the first time -- and often for the last time.

Cyril Beaumont wrote of her -- "All her dancing was distinguished by its grace, airiness, and absence of visible effort. It was sincere, refined, marked by a vivid sense of style-atmosphere, and a genuine and deeply felt reverence for the poetry of movement."

On the bitterly cold morning of January 24th, 1931, Novikoff arranged a memorial service at the Old Russian Church on Chicago's Leavitt Street (the church designed by Louis Sullivan), and we all attended, carrying candles and following a chanting priest around the church from altar to altar, occasionally kneeling on the cold floor.

But for our generation, at least, this was not the end of the great Pavlova's career; for we had photographed her in our minds at *the still point*.

EPIGRAPH

Just as the sound of music appeals to the ear, in the same way movement appeals to the eye of the spectator. Most of the great moments in dance history are preserved only by romancing, memory, and the written word. Photographs, art work and engravings all give us some idea of the appearance of the dancers of the past, some notion of their style, their costumes and character, but the really important thing in ballet is the movement itself.

The dance is purely a momentary art, lasting only for the moment it passes before your eyes. Before this moment, all the thought, creation and preparation by choreographer and performer; then that moment: <u>the still point</u> that flashes before the viewer's eyes and is photographed in the mind of the spectator. At the very next instant it has passed, never to be seen exactly the same again unless filmed by a motion picture camera.

WALTER CAMRYN

On June 8, 1989, I had the privilege and pleasure of having lunch with Ruth Page and Sheila Malkind. Her beautiful apartment, adorned with art pieces and the presence of sea shells filling the window sills, gave a feeling of serenity and peace, offering a close relationship with Lake Michigan, which stretched out far into the distance. As Ms. Page leafed through a book of Anna Pavlova, she paused for a moment, pointing to Pavlova's picture and said: "This is how I remember her." With her hand gently resting on the book, she seemed to reminisce for an instant, as I tried to imagine what was the start of her long and glorious career in dance.

In fact, Ms. Page was one of the first pioneers of this century whose influence on the dance world will be felt forever.

Photo by : Sheila Malkind

WALTRAUD G. KARKAR

To get to my first dance lessons in Darmstadt, Germany, I remember going through a beautiful park that once was the private property of the Royal Family, Ernst-Ludwig von Hessen. The park was one of my favorite places. I took it as a shortcut to the theatre. Graceful swans bathed in the sun and stretched their wings under the often bright blue sky. The park's many ponds were banked by an assortment of flowers that filled the air with a fresh scent.

I was fascinated by a monument of the little Princess Elizabeth von Hessen, a sculptured head with long curls. My grandmother told me that young Elizabeth met with a tragic death in 1903 in Russia at age seven, only a little younger than I was at the time.

Surrounding the park, guarding the serenity of those within, was a stone wall with a large wrought iron gate. Just beyond the gate and next to the statue, stood the Landes Theater Darmstadt, where I took lessons. Most of it had been damaged during World War II, so, sadly, at that time, it was mostly used for rehearsals for the opera and ballet.

I would make my way through a side door and up the narrow, musty-smelling stone steps that wound around to the third floor dressing room. Whenever ballet rehearsals ran late, we had the thrill of sharing the same dressing room with the professional dancers. As we put on our technique slippers, we watched in awe as they removed their stained and sweaty point shoes. It was such an honor to share a bench with these dancers I admired.

When I was thirteen, my mother bought me a subscription ticket for performances at the Orangerie Theatre in the old city of Darmstadt. Until I left Darmstadt at age eighteen, I sat in seat G54 the first Thursday of every month to see, alone, opera, ballet and plays. During that period, I also performed with a group of young dancers, very similar to Joffrey II. We were invited to dance in many beautiful opera houses, gaining excellent experience.

After I moved to America, I married Jack, an economist by profession, who continues to be supportive of my artistic pursuits. We, together have been able to bring ballet to thousands of school children rarely exposed to dance. We often took advantage of being pioneers and tried innovative approaches, such as dancing on wrestling mats in a public plaza.

The years I have spent in Wausau, from 1969 to the present, have been most challenging. I have raised five children, and as luck would have it, three of them loved to dance. When our son Patrik became a scholarship student at the Joffrey School of Ballet, it gave me a golden opportunity to be in the big city, to take as many classes as possible, and to watch many wonderful teachers. Although we have lived in one place, it seemed as though we were always on the move, traveling long hours to attend performances by every major company in the United States and abroad.

Our travels and our love for dance inspired us to build a school in 1969. We now have a spacious building with ultra-modern facilities.

My crowning achievement came when Madame Elvira Vecsey, prima ballerina and, later, ballet mistress of the Budapest Opera House in Hungary gave me private lessons for six years. She taught me the Russian Vaganova Grades.

With financial assistance from the Central Wisconsin Ballet Foundation and the Wausau Performing Arts Foundation, we have been able to invite choreographers and dancers from all over the world, notably: Joan Lawson from the Royal Ballet in England; Charthel Arthur, formerly of the Joffrey Ballet; Edward Villella, formerly of the New York City Ballet and now with the Miami Ballet; Basil Thompson, formerly of the American Ballet Theatre, Joffrey Ballet, and, presently, with the Milwaukee Ballet.

Our performances have blossomed over the years. We stage *The Nutcracker* every December, and spring and summer performances of such productions as: *La Fille Mal Gardée*, *Viva Vivaldi*, *Pas de Quatre*, excerpts from *A Chorus Line*, *A Midsummer Night's Dream*, excerpts from *The Music Man* and many others. With each successive performance, we've reached new audiences. Matinee performances of the *Nutcracker* attract children from as far as a hundred miles away.

With the renovation of the old Opera House in Wausau, a dream came true. I now have a beautiful place for my dancers to perform and to present touring dance companies. The interior colors of beige, red and gold match the once majestic theatre of Darmstadt, where I studied so many years ago. Here in Wausau, Wisconsin, I am able to recreate those first impressions that kindled my love for dance.

The Old Landes Theatre, Darmstadt, Germany

The Orangerie

219

Index